MORE
MAPLE HILL STORIES

MORE
MAPLE HILL STORIES

By Roderick Turnbull

Illustrated by Joseph Bohler

THE LOWELL PRESS/KANSAS CITY, MISSOURI

MORE
MAPLE HILL STORIES

Dedication

This book is dedicated to all those older folks who like to reminisce about the days on the farm and the little country town when this country was progressing from the horse and buggy to the motor car, from mud roads to paved highways, from the binder to the combine and from the coal oil lamp to the electric light;

And, to those younger folks who enjoy reading about how their parents and grandparents lived in those good old days.

ROD TURNBULL

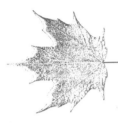

Foreword

The Maple Hill Stories are an important and vivid record of a time that will never come again, and thus they are an American treasure.

As agricultural editor of *The Kansas City Star,* and before that as editor of the *Weekly Star Farmer,* Rod Turnbull won high esteem and national recognition with his comment and analysis in the field of agriculture. Yet he will be remembered longest, I think, for putting Maple Hill, Kansas, on the literary map.

Most of us look back at childhood, or at least some of those long-ago-years, as a happy time. Nowadays that feeling has mushroomed into a cult of nostalgia. Things left behind from the "good old days," culled from attic, basement and barn, have become valuable, more costly often than the newest possessions. And along with the antiques, there is a new value placed on old memories.

Long before this development, Rod Turnbull, an

excellent reporter with a gift of memory and a mastery of words, realized the importance of preserving how it was to live in a small Kansas town during most of the first three decades of this century. Out of his memories came the Maple Hill Stories.

Blessed with a boyhood which embraced both the joys of a small town and the farms nearby, his Maple Hill recollections have a three-fold appeal. For those who were "big city kids," and never knew those delights of the small town, there is envy of such a pleasant childhood. There is an appeal as well for those who grew up in similar circumstances, yet do not have his wonderful talent for recalling how it was, and just as important, the ability to tell us today how it was then. And for the younger generation, who never knew those simpler days, there is the special benefit of words that capture and communicate the heritage of a historic era in the Middle West.

When Rod Turnbull retired from *The Star* in 1970, there was one job he did not want to leave behind, and his colleagues agreed with him. The Maple Hill Stories should continue in the paper. So they have, and with each of his reminiscences, there is the welcome accolade of telephone calls and letters of praise.

In this foreword to the second volume of Maple Hill Stories, I will echo that message from his readers to the author: "Tell us more."

Kansas City, Missouri   PAUL V. MINER
September 1, 1974   President of *The Star*

Contents

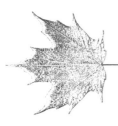

1   *"Hard Life" Was Fun*   2
2   *Hardships? Not Really*   8
3   *Each New Season Welcomed*   14
4   *Road Drags*   18
5   *Pride, Not Prestige*   28
6   *The First Cars*   34
7   *"Free Air"*   42
8   *Cars "Fully Stripped"*   48
9   *Yesterday's Sounds*   54
10 *When Eating Was Fun*   62
11 *Cow Pasture Baseball*   70
12 *Thrills and Terror When Fire Struck Town*   76
13 *Barefoot 'n Fancy Free*   86
14 *Nature's Cooling Breezes*   94
15 *Watermelon, Chicken and Summer*   100
16 *Summer's Best Treat*   106
17 *Canning for the Winter*   110
18 *New Sidewalks*   118

19 *Boys and Boats*   124
20 *Before the Combine*   134
21 *Threshing Days*   142
22 *Fun on the Farm*   150
23 *Riding the Caboose*   160
24 *First Long Pants*   168
25 *Walnuts, Food and Fun*   174
26 *Huntin' Dogs*   178
27 *Out-Sitting the Squirrel*   182
28 *The Old Stone Fence*   188
29 *Candidates Were Safe in Maple Hill*   194
30 *The First Armistice Day*   200
31 *Dressing the Turkey*   206
32 *Bounty on the Table*   214
33 *Country Store at Christmas Time*   222
34 *Electricity Changed Rural Life*   228
35 *The Gift Lamp*   236
36 *Mothers Made the Sunday School*   244
37 *Hard Work for Mothers*   252
38 *Mud Is Still Mud*   262
39 *The Versatile Nail Keg*   270
40 *Many Ways To Get Rid of Ashes*   278
41 *Railroads Sustained Small Towns*   284
42 *Cautious Courting*   294
43 *Luncheon Circuit Notes*   302

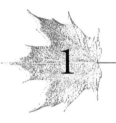

"Hard Life" Was Fun

1

SAVE fuel! Save energy! This was the government's plea the winter of 1973-74 because America was experiencing its first fuel shortage. People were advised not to burn Christmas lights.

A Christmas without the colorful electric lights?

Well, it happened before and we lived through it. In fact, when I was a boy at Maple Hill, Kansas, nobody had electrically lighted ornaments either on their Christmas trees or on their houses for the very simple reason we didn't have electric power.

I like the Christmas lights. I think they are beautiful, but I'll admit we enjoyed Christmas and the holidays just as much without them at Maple Hill.

The fact is most of the discomforts with which we are threatened because of a shortage of oil were a normal part of our lives at Maple Hill. And, I hasten to add, we were not pioneers, nor did we regard our way of life as one of hardships. For that day, the Turnbull family lived well.

I would neither suggest nor urge that we go back to that way of living, happy as it was, because in my opinion, every improvement, particularly those made possible by electricity, has been wonderful. This is especially true for mothers who used to have the burden of running homes without any of the gadgets which make the work so much easier today. Washing on a scrub board and hanging the clothes on a line outdoors to freeze is one example. Of course, big cities got electricity long before the lines reached little towns like Maple Hill and the farms.

But the way we lived proves you can get along if you have to without many of the so-called necessities of today. Of course we didn't miss things we never had.

We are getting all kinds of advice now on how to save fuel. Shut the heat off in rooms which are not being used, we are told.

That would have been useless advice in our Maple Hill home because when evening came, we had heat only in the front room. The fire in the kitchen range was allowed to die out after supper, to be rekindled the first thing in the morning.

The whole family spent the evening in the front room enjoying the warmth of the Round Oak stove. We had our best coal oil lamp in the center of the library table. I assume it was called a library table because that was the home's reading center. Everybody sat close by because the lamp's light was limited.

About the time I was of teen age, my father bought a

Coleman gasoline lamp, the kind with two mantles which had to be pumped up with air at intervals. It gave off a fine, white light making reading easier.

We took the *Saturday Evening Post, Colliers* and the Topeka papers, which, along with an occasional popular book such as those written by Zane Grey, kept us occupied. I don't want to indicate that we spent all our time reading, especially my brothers and I, but whatever we did do on a cold winter night was done in that one room.

Meanwhile, upstairs where we slept, it was freezing.

Virtually all homes in Maple Hill were the same way. The Weavers and the Frank Adams family had coal furnaces. My Uncle Al Romick had a big wood-burning furnace in the cellar that would take a log as heavy as a man could lift.

Our school also had a furnace. The school was a square, two-story frame structure. On zero days when the wind was blowing hard, the furnace just could not get the job done. If our teacher observed that some of the pupils were shivering, she'd announce we'd take a few minutes to warm up with exercises. We'd all stand between the aisles of desks and do such things as clap hands over our heads, jump up and down and swing our bodies from one side to the other.

This wasn't any hardship. Anything to get our minds off studies for a few minutes was welcomed. So we shivered easily, even though every boy and girl in class was wearing long underwear.

We're being told that sleeping two persons to a bed is warmer than sleeping alone. Of course, it is.

4

When my brother Bernard and I were real small, on an extremely cold night, I would sleep with my father because I was the oldest and Bernard slept with our mother. It was the only way they could be sure we would keep warm.

In the mornings Bernard and I would laugh and boast about who slept the warmest. Again, it wasn't any hardship. We thought it was a treat to get to sleep with Dad and Mom.

After the third brother, Don, was born, he slept between our mother and father while Bernard and I slept in our own room. We'd undress down to our long underwear in front of the stove in the front room, stand close to the stove until our underwear got as hot as we could stand it, then make a quick dash upstairs to dive under the heavy layers of covers.

If it was one of those awfully cold nights, our mother would heat a couple of flat-irons, wrap them in a piece of an old blanket and put them under the covers at the foot of the bed.

We did, of course, keep a fire in the big stove in the front room which could be stimulated in a hurry in the morning by opening up the drafts.

Advice also is being given today to keep the level of heat in the water heater at only the minimum.

Here, again, this would have been useless advice in our old home, but we sure could have demonstrated how to go easy on the use of hot water.

A big tea kettle was an absolute necessity in the rural home. It was the main source of hot water.

At our home, my father was the first to get up in the morning. He had a routine which varied only with the weather. On a winter morning, the first task was to open the draft in the big stove in the front room, shake the ashes from the fire chamber and add new coal. By the time the rest of the family arrived downstairs, the stove would be red hot.

Next, my father put some corn cobs (which we boys had brought in the night before) into the kitchen range, dashed them with coal oil (kerosene) and set them ablaze. When the cobs started to burn, he added coal and in no time at all the stove was roaring.

Then he put on the kettle filled with water. And it stayed on the stove until we went to bed at night.

If the weather outside was extremely cold, the first warm water from the kettle went to prime the kitchen pump. We had a cistern pump in the kitchen, a luxury not too many families enjoyed. But on a real cold night, we had to drain the water from the pump's cylinder to keep it from freezing and breaking the pipes. Thus, when the cylinder was empty, it was necessary to pour some water in the top of the pump in the morning to get the suction cups operating again.

Water from the cistern obviously would be cold. Boiling kettle water mixed in a basin with water from the cistern was used to wash your hands and face.

We also enjoyed the luxury of what was called a reservoir on the kitchen range. This was sort of a tank on the range which held about five gallons of water. This water would be warmed up (it never boiled) by the fire in the range.

Water from the kettle also sufficed for washing the dishes morning, noon and night. But on Monday wash days, when more hot water was needed, our mother heated water in a big copper boiler on top of the range.

Looking back, it now is obvious to me that hot water was somewhat of a luxury and we probably got by on an ordinary day with two buckets full. Saturday nights and on wash days it took more.

When there was no hot water, we washed our hands with water straight from the pump.

If anyone does not realize what a luxury warm water is, he should try that some time on a cold winter's day.

The government asks us to use our cars less.

We didn't have a gasoline shortage when I was a boy, but we didn't use a lot of gasoline, either, especially in winter time. It was the weather and bad roads which "rationed" the use of our car.

We bought our first car, an Overland, the summer of 1916. That winter, when the snow and cold arrived, we drained the radiator, put all four wheels on the car on jacks to take the weight off the tires and took the battery out to put it behind the kitchen range.

When we wanted to use the car we had to put the battery back in, let the wheels down from the jack and then fill the radiator with boiling water from the kettle. One of us would push down on the starter while another whirled the crank. If she started, we were ready to go. Nobody had to tell us to go easy on the use of the car. In fact, in cases of icy or muddy roads, it was easier to walk.

But we lived through it and I never have had a car the possession of which has given me a thrill equal to that 1916 Overland. Maybe experiences make us all appreciate things just a little more again.

Hardships? Not Really

2

Much is being said these days suggesting that one cause of juvenile delinquency and the unrest among teen-agers is that they don't experience the hardships that were common-place for previous generations and that they don't have responsibilities forced upon them. In other words, life is just too easy.

Perhaps there is truth in these assumptions, but I am glad the same criteria didn't hold when I was a boy.

Undoubtedly, we would have been a ruined generation because as far as I can recall, we had no hardships—that is, recognized hardships. Nor did responsibilities weigh heavy on our shoulders. We grew up, perhaps naively, seeking to have as much fun as we could and assuming that at adulthood we would go to work to earn a living.

What are hardships? This is rather hard to define. Certainly, you don't miss something you never had.

As an example, when I was a boy in Maple Hill we didn't have air-conditioned homes. In fact, we didn't even have electric fans.

To be more specific, we didn't have electricity.

We could have used an electric fan, but I can't say we suffered without it. Among the most satisfactory of experiences was to pick a spot in the house where there was a draft and lie down for a snooze after dinner.

I'm speaking about the noonday dinner. We never had luncheon snacks. After working from 7 a. m. to noon in the blacksmith shop, my father expected his meat and potatoes at noon just the same as at supper time. He came home for dinner, of course.

And, after this full noon meal, it was customary to lie down on the floor with just a pillow under your head for a few minutes' rest before going back to work. Farmers did the same thing. It was believed you rested better for a brief period on the floor rather than on the davenport or a bed.

I contend that the discontinuance of the after-dinner (noon) nap is one of America's great losses.

We improvised at night to get the coolest sleeping spot. On real hot nights, our parents had pallets on the floor where there was a good draft. My brother, Bernard, and I had a sanitary couch on the front porch—a sanitary couch being a metal frame affair which could be made into a bed by lifting up the sides. Why it was called "sanitary" I never knew.

We liked sleeping on the porch so well that we often started in early spring and sometimes would get caught in the last snowfall. This was our idea of "pioneering." We always ran around barefoot in the snow once each spring, too, just to prove we were tough.

There's nothing more delightful than being awakened out on the porch at dawn by the cooing of turtle doves, pulling the sheet over your head to keep out the light of the rising sun and going back to sleep.

With no electricity, we had no water systems in our homes. We were fortunate at our house because we had a good well and a cistern pump. We also had a good well at the blacksmith shop. Maple Hill had a town pump in the center of Main Street at the principal downtown intersection (come to think of it, the only downtown intersection).

On a hot day, we thought the finest thing going was a cold drink from a good well. You always pumped out enough water to make sure any that had been standing in the pipes was gone and that what you were drinking was coming from the depths of the well.

Actually, the only hardship experienced as far as drinking wcter was concerned was when we went to Topeka or Manhattan and had to drink what we thought was the "awful" city water. Drinking fountains in those days were not refrigerated and the city water in the summer was practically tepid. It also had a funny taste to us. We hardly could wait until we got back home to get a good drink from a well.

We had a good well, too, at the Maple Hill school. It provided a few moments reprieve when the bell sounded ending recess. All the boys playing in the school yard ran to the well for a "life-saving" drink before going back to classes. This was accomplished by someone pumping furiously while the others took

10

turns cupping their hands as they hurriedly quaffed the cold water.

Frankly, a well pump could get tiresome under certain circumstances. For instance, if you had to pump enough water to quench the thirst of a herd of cows. That's why windmills were so popular.

Pumping water with a "force" pump through a hose to a motor car was a tiring chore, too. Our pump at the blacksmith shop was of the "force" type. This meant the valves were so arranged that water could not drain back into the well. Each push on the pump handle forced the water out the spout rather than "lifting" it out. The result was you could operate with a hose if you had the strength to keep pumping.

My brothers and I distinctly disliked the job of washing the family car with the hose at the force pump. Obviously, the one on the pump had the hardest task. The problem was solved by not washing the car very often.

Speaking of cars, we liked to drive them just as much as teen-agers today. However, few, if any, teen-agers in our town owned their own car. Most families had cars, but parents weren't as lenient as now.

There were obvious reasons. Even our fathers didn't drive cars as much then as now. Mud roads didn't lend themselves to traveling as do today's interstate highways. Motor car tires (ordinary guaranteed 3,000 miles, deluxe 5,000) did not suggest casual use. Any teen-ager attempting a rubber burning start was considered downright silly.

The fact was, getting to drive the family car was a

treat or a privilege. My brother Bernard and I (at age 12 or 13) would vie to see who got to back the car out of the garage. If we drove to town (two blocks), one drove down and the other back. The issue was decided before we started, with our mother usually gaining some concession before we were permitted to leave.

It was a real treat when we were allowed to drive to St. Marys, 10 miles away, to attend a Sunday night picture show. In fact, even getting to attend the show was a privilege because our parents weren't too friendly to Sunday night shows.

St. Marys was the only town in our area that had movies. It was a big deal when both you and your date could get permission to go to St. Marys and you also could get the family car, even if you didn't have the money to buy her an ice cream sundae.

When my brother, Don, came along, 10 years younger than I, the use of the family car was far more common for high school boys than it had been for me. Things changed quickly. I marveled at how my father let Don drive to basketball games at Eskridge, Alma, Rossville and St. Marys as if it were routine. But they had started to gravel county roads by then.

It was the custom in our town for boys of 11 and 12 to start working for farmers and ranchers in the hay fields at $1 a day. As we got a little older, we worked in the harvest and made as high as $4 or $5 a day.

A boy was said to be doing well when he made enough to buy his school clothes in the fall. Downtown on Saturday nights, it was a proud mother who could say, "Our boys have saved enough this summer to buy their school shoes, shirts and trousers."

12

The truth was, we weren't very affluent, but it didn't take a whole lot of money to get along. Regular "allowances" were unheard of at the time.

The work in the hay fields and in the wheat harvest was hard, but since everybody was doing it, we didn't complain. And it wasn't very steady work. You put up a cutting of alfalfa hay and you had to wait a few weeks for another crop to mature. You couldn't work when it was raining.

On a rainy day, we'd gather downtown at the blacksmith shop or spend the morning listening to farmers swap stories in the barbershop. Farmers and other day laborers would be idled by the rain, so they would use the time to get a haircut and a shave.

Iron pegs always were in place near the blacksmith shop for games of horse shoes. Anybody, from boys to old men, could get a game going at any time. We boys would play horse shoes until we tired of the game then we'd mosey down to Mill Creek for a swim.

We certainly had nothing that could be called supervised recreation in the summer. There was the annual Sunday school picnic, which featured lots of good food, free ice and pop. The Modern Woodmen had a picnic each year and usually some town in the area had a picnic, baseball game and dance on the Fourth of July.

Other than for these events, we were on our own. And we managed to provide our own entertainment without parental supervision. We didn't have Boy Scouts or 3 & 2 baseball teams but we did a lot of traipsing around the creeks and woods and baseball was played, morning, afternoon and evenings.

Each New Season Welcomed

3

WHEN I was a boy growing up my companions and I thoroughly enjoyed each season of the year, but we got tired of each one and were early in welcoming a change.

Thus, in late January we began to get bored with winter and started to anticipate spring. By late January, winter sports had run their course. Mill Creek seldom froze over in February so that we had to do our skating during January. Actually, while there was no fixed weather pattern, most of our ice skating came around Christmas time or the first week in January.

There was something about February snows that provided them with less appeal than those earlier in the winter for coasting on the big hill west of town. If conditions were right, we'd get a crowd on the hill some evening or some Sunday afternoon, but by February, coasting day after day had lost some of its enchantment.

Probably the greatest change came in hunting, which was our primary winter entertainment. We started hunting squirrels in October. With the first cold snap of the fall, we began to rout rabbits out of the brush piles and corn shocks. Also, we started setting our traps for skunks, possums, raccoons, civet cats and muskrats.

By late January, we were tired of getting up at daylight to run traplines before school. The profit from the sale of the furs never was quite as large as we had hoped. Somehow, with few exceptions, the prices we received always were at the low end of the scale quoted on the lists sent out by the fur companies.

And in late January, we had been told the rabbits had started breeding and the females probably would be carrying a brood of young ones.

Frankly, February didn't have much to offer except that it bridged the gap between the best part of the winter and spring.

So, we started thinking about spring. We spent our Saturdays hanging around my father's blacksmith shop, welding pieces of old iron together on an idle forge, sharpening our pocket knives on oil stones and listening to farmers talk about what they intended to do just as soon as they could get their plows in the ground. The first crop to be sown would be oats and the onset of spring became a practical fact when the oats were in the ground. Sometimes this happened the first week in March.

For the boys, spring was officially inaugurated either the Sunday before Easter or on Easter itself. It was a tradition in our town (that's what we claimed anyhow) that boys went swimming in Mill Creek on one of these Sundays.

Mill Creek was particularly inviting in early spring—except for the temperature. The water was exceptionally clear and you could see the gravel bottom close to the shore.

After church and Sunday dinner, the boys would wander down to the creek. If it were a nice sunshiny day, we left no doubts that we were going to jump into the creek at once. We'd take off our clothes on a gravel bar and start the process of determining who would be first. Some villain would have the nerve to cup up a handful of icy water and toss it at our naked bodies. A couple tricks like this and there was no doubt who was going to be the first man in. We'd grab the villain and throw him in. In the struggle, we'd all be in the water about the same time. And just as fast, we'd all be out again. That would end the first swim of the spring, and the tradition had been maintained.

We'd go home and brag that we had gone swimming and our mothers would contend that it was a wonder we didn't all take down with pneumonia. But if anyone ever caught a cold, I never heard of it.

Fishing, for us, was a warm weather sport. We didn't take our poles or trot lines to Mill Creek until the weather was pleasant. Nor did we ever fish in the winter. It was said that the time for fishing had arrived when the earthworms became abundant in the gardens. Therefore, when you were spading the garden and you found big fat, juicy worms, you knew catfish would bite.

At our school, the spring track season opened with a

cross-country run or fox-and-goose chase. This was the teacher's way of finding out our different abilities. Since we were a small school, every boy took part in preparing for track meets even though only the best might be entered in the annual county competition at Alma, the county seat.

For the fox-and-goose chase, two boys would lead out across country carrying an arm load of paper. At intervals, they (the geese) would tear pieces of the paper and drop them on the ground. The rest of us (the fox) were supposed to follow the trail and attempt to catch them. Eventually all of us would end up back at the school absolutely exhausted.

Along with track practice, we had spring baseball. This was living. We liked nothing at school—including track—as well as baseball. Everybody had to participate or else we didn't have enough for two teams. A team didn't have to have nine men to fill it out. We could do with a few less than nine.

But summer was best of all. No school. In theory, at least, just fun.

Then came August, which was a little like February. Dog days had set in. The water in Mill Creek was warm and there was a green scum over even the deepest holes. We'd swim below the riffles in the evenings rather than take a bath at home. We no longer cared about sitting on the bank with a fishing pole in our hands. In fact, the idea of school didn't seem so bad.

Summer was over and we were looking forward to fall.

Road Drags

4

Among the pleasant recollections of living in my old home town is that of walking barefoot on the country roads just after they had been "dragged." A road was dragged as soon as possible after the earth dried following a rain. The dirt was smooth and soft and felt good to your feet.

Another pleasure was taking a ride in the motor car on a summer's evening on a freshly dragged road—the smoothest ride you'd ever experience in the days when paved roads were a rarity, actually nonexistent in rural areas.

My father, mother, brothers and I would take advantage of the smooth road just for the ride to "cool off" after a hot day. We'd have the top down on our Overland touring car as we rode along in pure luxury enjoying the cool air and the farm scenery—not going anyplace in particular, just riding.

Among recollections not so pleasant are those of

those same roads when they were muddy and full of ruts, rough and difficult to travel by car, buggy or wagon. Dirt roads were rough more often than they were smooth, which was why it was such a pleasure to enjoy a brief period of excellence after dragging.

In dry times, the road surface might stay relatively smooth for weeks, but the earth would become so hard it wasn't the same as that period shortly after a rain.

Today, with all the paved highways and even gravel-surfaced country roads, it is rather difficult to recall what a barrier bad roads were to transportation only a relatively short time ago. Rapid growth in the number of motor cars, plus the development of mechanized road-building equipment, has in one lifetime "taken us out of the mud," a phrase used far more some years ago than now for the simple reason that it's now an ccomplished fact. Once it was a dream.

One of the devices that helped to start road improvement was the drag.

The drag was a device, pulled by horses, to smooth the road's surface and to push the loose earth toward the center of the road to make a "crown." With the crown in the center, water from rains flowed to ditches at the sides of the road. Because the water flowed away, rather than soaking in, the road dried faster.

My father made road drags in the blacksmith shop. But he didn't invent the device. In recent years, I have read that the road drag may have been created by a Missouri farmer named D. Ward King. Stories about road improvement in the early 1900s refer to the introduction of the King drag and I assume this is the one.

Wayne E. Fuller's book, which tells about the creation of the rural mail route service, mentions the King road drag and says that King showed his drag to a group of farmers at Wellsville, Kansas, in 1906. So impressed were they that within a week about 20 drags were built and all but two miles of a 25-mile rural mail route out of town had been dragged.

The King road drag was a simple device, just a split log, half of it fastened solidly about 3 feet in front of the other. Any farmer could make one cheaply.

"But if it were pulled over a muddy road, especially after a rain, it smoothed the road and rounded it toward the center in such a way as to cause it to drain more easily," Fuller writes. "When the road dried it became quite hard and farmers learned that a fairly decent road could be made if the dragging process were repeated several times."

The drags made in the blacksmith shop at Maple Hill were an improvement over the King device. They were made with two 14-foot, 2x12-inch planks, one set behind the other. Big iron bolts, made on the anvil, were used to make the drag frame sturdy. These drags usually were pulled with a four-horse team and the driver stood on a board between the two planks.

Steel plates on the lip edges of the planks not only helped cut clods of dirt, but made the planks last longer.

The wood drag was followed by a grader with a steel blade that could be adjusted up and down. But the device still was pulled by a four-horse team.

A good maintenance man managed to get to his road at the proper time after a rain. A drag couldn't be operated in the mud, of course, but it didn't do much good after the ground became dry and hard. There was, therefore, a proper but brief period when the ground was dry enough for the vehicle, but soft enough to work well. You could tell by the road whether a maintenance man knew his business.

Fortunately for Maple Hill, there was a wealthy rancher, W. J. Tod, who lived about a mile from town and liked to keep the road to his place in good shape.

Mr. Tod drove to town every day for his mail and he often also had business at the bank or the depot. The ranch had its own drag and plenty of big horses to pull it. After every rain, a ranch employee was on the road with the drag at just the right time. As a result, it was the smoothest road around and for an evening's drive, we always took the "Tod road."

The wonder to me is that the road drag is of such recent origin, assuming King did develop it in the early 1900s.

However, reports on road work in Missouri, Kansas and other farm states indicate not only how little was done to make roads passable in those days, but how little farmers or townspeople actually could do with the horse-drawn machinery available.

Mostly, a road was just a stretch of land between two fences left to the devices of nature. It was passable to buggies and wagons, but nothing else.

The old Tenth Street Road (named because it started on Tenth Street in Topeka) wasn't passable even for wagons in bad weather in the vicinity of Maple Hill. The same road now is I-70 across Wabaunsee County, and I'm virtually certain that more

21

money was spent building the interchange at Maple Hill than had previously been spent on all roads around the town in history.

The motor car forced road improvement. But the cars and their drivers took a lot of beating before the improvements came.

I have often been asked, after the appearance of a Maple Hill story in *The Star,* if I was acquainted with people who lived in Eskridge, another Wabaunsee County town about 20 miles over the hills to the south.

I didn't know many Eskridge people for the simple reason that we seldom drove there unless we were in a spell of dry weather and had good tires on our car. You didn't want to get caught out in those hills in the mud.

This all changed rapidly within a few years as the roads were either sanded or graveled and later paved.

The *1898 Yearbook* published by the U. S. Department of Agriculture has many pages devoted to road improvement. In one place, the book relates that steel-track wagon road still was in the experimental stage.

This was a scheme, apparently tried first in Ohio, of laying flat steel tracks on ordinary roadbeds. At first it was thought a wood foundation was needed for the tracks, but this was considered too costly. So, eventually, a contract was let for 500 feet of steel track on a road just south of Cleveland. The steel plates were imbedded in concrete.

The idea was that only the wheels of the wagon would use the tracks. Pictures are used in the *Year-*

book to illustrate that while it took 20 horses to pull a load of 11 tons on an ordinary road, one horse could pull the same tonnage on a steel track road.

The construction cost of a short section of track was $1 a foot. Test tracks were laid in several other states about the same time, all for very short distances.

All these efforts were experimental at the time and were treated so by the *1898 Yearbook.* Nothing is said as to why the idea apparently came to naught.

The same *Yearbook,* however, in another chapter, comments that "the road is a type of civilized society" and it adds, "the condition of the public roads in the United States probably is worse than in any other civilized country in the world."

One reason for these poor roads, the book explains, was a lack of knowledge on the part of many road officials on the primary principles of road construction. Poor roads, the book admonishes, are a "detriment to social communication, education and religion" as well as a hindrance to marketing.

The *Yearbook* makes these comments:

"Many roads in this country were originally laid out without any attention to general topography, and in most cases followed the settlers' path from cabin to cabin, the pig's trail from his favorite nut-producing trees to his wallow in the mud and water of the swamps, or the boundary line of farms regardless of grades or direction. Most of them remain today where they were originally located, and where untold labor, expense and energy have been wasted in trying to haul over them and in endeavoring to improve their deplorable condition.

"It is a great error to continue to follow these primitive paths with public highways. The proper thing to do is to call in a good road engineer and have the location so changed as to throw the roads around the ends or along the sides of the steep hills and ridges instead of continuing to go over them, or in raising the roads up on dry, solid ground, instead of splashing through the mud and water of the bogs and creeks of lowlands.

"If the road goes over the hill when it might go around, the labor and expense put upon it are absolutely wasted, and the sooner its direction is changed the better . . . In laying out a road, straightness always should be sacrificed to obtain a comparatively level surface. . . There is no objection to an absolutely straight road, but graceful and natural curves conforming to the lay of the land add beauty to the landscape besides enhancing the value of the property . . . Good roads should wind around hills instead of running over them."

The article goes on to explain how horses just couldn't pull big loads uphill; therefore it was common sense to make the road as level as possible.

For one thing, the advice in the *Yearbook* helps explain why it was, when we finally got around to paving roads in this part of the country, that nearly all of them followed routes around the hills and over the ridges. Relatively quickly they were all outmoded and the main highways were made as straight as possible, through the hills when necessary rather than around them. The horse and buggy days finally were over.

Incidentally, in a chapter on road maintenance, the

Yearbook advises that holes, ruts or puddles in dirt roads should be filled in. A rake should be used freely, it was said, in removing stones, lumps and ridges. This would indicate that the drag was not commonly available in 1898.

The 1911 report of the Missouri State Department of Agriculture contains an article by Curtis Hill, state highway engineer. He mentioned that state and county highway engineers worked with the Cape Girardeau Normal to put on a drag demonstration in 1909.

"There were few present who ever had seen a drag used on a gravel road," Hill said, "and the demonstration was given before a skeptical audience."

But the demonstration was effective because it led to the use of the drag later on many roads in the community.

A far more impressive demonstration was conducted in 1910 when the state highway engineer and the Frisco railroad ran a special five-car "good roads" train across the state from St. Louis by way of Springfield and Lamar. The train carried one baggage car and four flat cars. The flat cars carried road-making machinery lent to the state by machinery companies.

The equipment included three wheel scrapers, two drag scrapers, one buck scraper, one four-horse roller, one road plow, three rooter plows, one big and one little road grader, one drag and all the double trees and neckyokes and other necessary attachments required.

The train made several stops at towns across the

state. All stops were from two to four days. The equipment would be unloaded and, during the days, road-building demonstrations would be put on. At night there would be meetings to promote good roads.

It was demonstrated in Franklin County, as an example, that a good natural country road could be built at a cost of about $324 a mile. Gravel was available in abundance, so the road could be surfaced with this material for an additional $700, or a total cost to the mile of about $1,000.

The main object of the whole trip was to arouse public interest in road improvement. Apparently at the time the state highway department either didn't have much authority or much money.

Hill concluded his report with these comments:

"The trip was put through for the express purpose of illustrating that more good can be accomplished by the state highway engineer by demonstration work than in any other way . . . It does seem to me that the few small demonstrations together with this one railroad trip, should convince anyone that, in addition to the expense of running the office, the state highway engineer should be supplied with money for road demonstrations and experimental work."

A contrast to this statement was the revelation a few years ago by the Missouri State Highway Commission that it had set aside $62,515,418 just for maintenance of the state's 33,000-mile highway network for the 1970-71 fiscal year.

What tremendous progress since the old King road drag!

Pride, Not Prestige

5

Much is said and written these days about "prestige" and "status symbols" as a motivating force in modern life. This is something that we apparently just hadn't heard about when I was a boy. Perhaps I was naive and didn't recognize something that existed only in adult or more alert minds, but of this I can be certain: As a boy I never heard of a "prestige item" and I don't believe any of the other youngsters did either.

Nobody, as far as I knew, built a two-car garage, installed a furnace, or bought any new gadget for the home with the idea that it denoted prestige. As far as the garage was concerned, many a family buying its first car didn't have any garage at all; they pulled the wagon out of the center runway of the barn or the machine shed, and that was the shelter the car got.

A barn, incidentally, and a machine shed, too, had one serious drawback as a good place to store the car.

They were open to the chickens, and chickens seemed to have a special liking for the car top and fenders as roosting places.

Our lack of appreciation or recognition of prestige didn't mean we failed to recognize value, quality and the like. It must have been we were more interested in other things—maybe just acquiring the things we actually needed. We didn't have the money to buy anything else. Or, we may have expressed our judgments in other ways.

For instance, we almost made a profession of not being "stuck up." Whether someone who was "stuck up" was seeking to suggest prestige, I wouldn't know.

There was one couple, for example, who had come to this country from England and they deplored the lack of culture in our town. The wife insisted that her son and daughter call her "mother." She also added "dear" to their names whenever she called them in from play, and they were supposed to return this sign of affection.

At that time, we called our parents, pop, papa and dad, and mom or mamma. We considered "mother" an affectation and this poor boy had an awful time on the school ground as we tantalized him with "mother dear" wants that, or "Have you asked mother dear if you can play?"

He finally lived it all down by running away and joining the Navy. I'm sure the mother never did understand what was wrong. She was trying hard to give her children a little something nicer—prestige, perhaps that the rest of us didn't have.

At the opposite end of the line as far as appellations

for our parents were concerned were terms used by the bigger boys and only the boldest of the younger ones. This was "the old man" and "the old lady."

It was fairly common among men to refer to their elderly fathers as "the old man," a shade less common to speak of their mothers as "the old lady." Among young fellows it was sort of a sign of independence to refer to "the old man." Among boys it was downright daring.

"If I ever hear you speak of me as the old lady, I'll tan you until you won't sit down for a week," my mother would say to me and my brothers. She must have been all of 35 or 36 at the time.

All our mothers worked hard. They baked bread, washed on a washboard or with hand-powered washing machines, cooked over coal stoves or coal oil ranges, killed and cleaned the chickens, canned fruit and vegetables, rendered lard at butchering time, and otherwise fulfilled every task necessary to feed and take care of the family. Work carried no stigma.

But even here, as I now recall, there were some few standards below which our mothers didn't want to stoop in the matter of work—which perhaps could be put in the category of prestige. Only the "poor" women had to chop their own stove wood.

My mother would say to us as we were pleading with her to let us go out to play instead of bringing in the wood, kindling or coal at the moment:

"Now, would you like to see your mother out there chopping wood and carrying it into the house like poor Mrs. so and so, while that nogood son of hers is out playing and her husband is spending all day loafing down town in front of the pool hall? I ask you, is that what you want people to see your mother doing?"

Of course, we didn't want to see such a terrible thing happen to our mother as that; so, reluctantly, we'd bring in enough wood or coal to keep the fires going. Most mothers I knew didn't have to chop wood.

If there was one situation the women dreaded, it was taking in washing.

"If anything happened to your father, I suppose I could take in washing," was a common thing for us youngsters to hear—not just at our house.

And there was more truth than poetry in this, because not many opportunities for jobs were open to women in our little town in those days. We didn't have social security, either.

But I don't know what we'd have done if a few women, often those with big families and used to hard work, had not "taken in washing." In times of illness, or when there was new baby in a house, the women who would "work out" were lifesavers.

Certain farmers around Maple Hill took great pride in their horses and without doubt this added to their prestige. It was sort of a mark of the kind of farmer and citizen a man was.

Jim Thompson's big matched Belgians were always sleek and fat, and the paint would shine on his green lumber wagon. J. W. Tod, the Scot rancher, one of the real well-to-do men in the community, drove a team of matched sorrels to his buggy. H. G. Adams, another big rancher, drove blacks. Steele Romick had a team of big white horses for his wagon. All of these were respected men.

It is difficult to categorize the motor car as a prestige item. When cars began to be a common vehicle around the country, surely everybody wanted one—that is, most everybody; some insisted they'd never take the place of a horse. Everybody wanted to get a ride in a car. It was a treat.

But mostly a car was a new and wonderful form of transportation. People didn't buy them to put on airs; they wanted a car because it meant they could get where they wanted to go so much faster.

Most of those purchased were Model T's, but actually there were so many kinds no one make carried prestige billing. Prestige was more likely to come if your car could take the Sells Hill south of town in high gear.

A car wasn't exactly a thing of beauty and there were certain things that could and did happen often to dampen the enthusiasm about prestige. Tires blew out and had to be repaired on the road and pumped up by hand. Connecting rods would burn out at the most inappropriate times. Brakes gave out and springs broke. None of these things ever happened to a horse.

I'm sure it wasn't for prestige that old Doc Taylor bought his first car, an Overland touring model. Doc was a farmer, not a physician. He soon learned the motor car had utility beyond its service as a method of transportation on the road. Occasionally Doc would drive the cows in from pasture with his car and he even tried pulling a mowing machine with it. People were horrified at the way old Doc treated that car.

Doc also was a little careless of the way he handled

his chewing tobacco and the port side of his car was evidence of his bad aim. Maybe he didn't allow for the wind.

When, some years later, we bought our first car and my father was taking a group of men, including Doc Taylor, to a lodge meeting, my mother warned she'd be furious if that car came home with "that horrid old tobacco juice all over the side." Dad laughed and said he'd rather it would be outside than in.

"When you chew tobacco, you've got to spit," he philosophized.

H. G. Adams bought the community's first Cadillac. H. G. wasn't in the habit of taking youngsters for a ride in his car, so we didn't envy that car too much. Mr. Tod was much slower about getting a car. He rather regretted giving up the dependable sorrels. After all, the roads being the way they were, having a team of horses around was still a sensible arrangement.

Prestige in our town was expressed also, but not by that term, in craftsmanship. There were stone masons whose quality of workmanship was known for miles around. Their buildings still stand. Farmers were proud of their straight rows of corn. Respect was shown a man who could put up a good stack of wheat. But if anyone had done anything just to suggest that he was a little higher up the social scale than other people, he would have been spotted a mile away.

The Rock Island railroad skirts Maple Hill on the southern edge. The whole town is to the north.

Maybe that was the reason we were not concerned about social prestige.

We all lived on the same side of the tracks.

The First Cars

6

PERHAPS the biggest thrill that comes to a boy or girl today is on the 16th birthday anniversary, when the youth passes the test that leads to a driver's license.

But it hasn't been so many years since a boy or girl, or adult for that matter, got a big thrill just in riding in a motor car. It was an experience you didn't forget when the doctor, banker or some other man of affluence in the community invited your family for a ride out into the country on a cool summer evening. Such a ride was a distinct privilege. You were even just a little bit afraid, as the car bounced over the rough roads, but who really cared? The wind blew in your face, new vistas came into view at the turn of every corner. This was excitement! You were *somebody* the next day when you could say casually, "Yea, I've ridden in one of those things."

In our town of Maple Hill, Doc Silver-

thorne had a big, seven-passenger Studebaker. Doc
Kemper bought an Overland. They were both touring
cars, of course, as there were no other kinds. H. G.
Adams got a Cadillac, but W. J. Tod, the other big
rancher, stuck to his team of sorrels. Rufe King, local
tough man, bought a used car which, if I recall
correctly, was a Stutz. Rufe managed to adjust the
carburetor so the thing would burn coal oil (kerosene)
and he was right proud of it, driving up to our house
one evening to show it off to my father. My father,
being the town's blacksmith, came just about as near
being what was known as a mechanic at the time as
any one else in the community.

"See, John," Rufe said to my father as the car stood
in the road in front of our house, "I start her on
gasoline, then run her on coal oil."

Billows of smoke were coming from the exhaust
pipe, but Rufe was happy. He sort of looked upon
himself as a mechanic, too. In fact, just about everybody did in those days. About all you needed to
qualify was a hammer and a wrench.

Rufe was able to start his car with gasoline and then
turn to coal oil by the simple process of filling petcocks
on the engine block with gasoline. You'd crank the car
while this gasoline drained into the cylinder head.
Once the engine was going, she'd draw the coal oil from
the fuel tank. If you'd keep the engine running fast
enough, the coal oil would work.

While garages were coming into vogue, and at
Maple Hill we didn't know whether the word should
be pronounced garAGE or GARage, the blacksmith
shop sufficed in a way of speaking for certain repairs.

On the rough roads, springs had a way of breaking. My father welded the broken pieces together on the anvil. Axles broke, too. If parts had to be ordered, sometimes a car would sit in the shop weeks at a time.

In fact, I got my first experience in driving by cranking up an old Overland which was waiting for repairs in the shop. I'd get the engine going, then throw the thing into low gear and crawl 6 to 10 feet forward. Then I'd reverse the process. Usually there'd be some other boy with me. We'd get this done a couple of times before my father would let a horse's foot down from his leather-aproned knee and order:

"You boys leave that car alone and stay away from it."

Of course we didn't stay away. Just sitting in the seats and holding onto the wheel was a thrill.

Then came the days of the cheaper Model T. Henry Ford said if enough cars were sold, buyers would get a rebate of $25. With nothing to go on but the memory of a boy, it seems to me the cars were selling at about $385. The rebate put them back to $360. Farmers and everybody began to get cars. In a few years there were Fords, Chevrolets, Studebakers, Overlands, Hudson Super Sixes, Chandlers, Auburns, Reos, Hupmobiles and everything else in the community.

Also, we acquired a garage in Maple Hill. My father let my grandfather run the shop while he went to Kansas City to take a six-week course in motor mechanics. After all, this thing looked as if it were going to be a real threat to the horse.

We got our first car in 1916—a dark green Overland, five-passenger touring car, model 83. That morning, as my brother Bernard and I went to work in the hayfields on Adams's ranch, we were hopeful. Our father was taking No. 40 on the Rock Island to Topeka, "just to look at cars." We had little confidence he actually would buy one.

That evening, as we were walking in from the ranch, a quarter of a mile away we spotted a new car sitting at the roadside in front of the house. We started running and didn't stop until we were in the car. Neighbors were around, too. This was an event.

The dealer from Topeka had shown my father how to drive the car on the trip out to Maple Hill. He took No. 36 back to Topeka and the car was all ours and we were on our own.

That evening, just as soon as supper was over, and before the sun went down, our family loaded into the car. Aunt Sofia and her children were with us. We were going around the square west of town.

Everything was lovely until we came to the corner where the road passes the Old Stone church and cemetery. Dad's coat sleeve hooked onto the hand gasoline lever as he started to turn the steering wheel. Instead of taking the corner, we went up the side of the road and stopped just short of the stone wall surrounding the graveyard. Mom and Aunt Sofia cried. Dad was pretty white. But no one was hurt and we drove on back to town.

With motor cars coming in the way they were, the future of blacksmithing was threatened. My father decided to buy the garage which was next door to the blacksmith shop. It was assumed that in addition to my intended career as a blacksmith, I had better learn something about cars, too. A hired man was put in charge of the garage and I was supposed to help and learn from experience.

Jim Hutchins was the hired man, a self-taught mechanic, slow in action, but capable, patient and kind. A principal job in those days was grinding the valves and scraping out the carbon.

Jim would say, "Roderick, my hands are too big to reach in there. See if you can't loosen that bolt." So I'd put my wrench on the bolt.

After we'd get the head off a car's engine and the pins out of the valve holders, Jim could tell me to go ahead and grind the valves. We had a hand tool we used on most cars, but on some models the tool didn't fit. In this case we used a carpenter's brace and special bit made by my father to turn the valve in its seat, where the rough edges were ground with a valve-grinding compound. It was a slow job and my father insisted that each valve be seated to perfection. I learned how to overhaul an engine.

We washed the family car—no others—at the blacksmith shop well, which had a force pump. This pump had a valve arrangement whereby water couldn't run back into the well, and every pump of the handle forced each gulp of water into the one ahead of it. Thus you had a continuous stream as long as you kept pumping. We bought a hose for the pump, which was supposed to make car washing easier. However, Bernard and I never peaceably settled who was to pump and who was to hold the hose. He being younger than I thought I should take the harder job. I, being older, thought I should command the hose.

We took turns, but still it was a tough job.

Obviously, Bernard and I learned to drive early. My big thrill came when my father let me drive out to Steele Romick's grove on Mill Creek to bring in some of the folks who had attended the summer's Sunday school picnic. Most of the crowd was coming back to town on a hayrack, but there were more than enough for one wagonload, hence the need to use the car. I'll never forget when we passed the wagon, how casual I tried to be, but how excited I was. My father never stopped cautioning me until we got past the wagon.

He was afraid I might run into it—or that the team would become frightened and run away. I don't recall any protest over the fact I was only 12 years old and barefoot.

We had a standing rule—which we knew would be enforced—that neither Bernard nor I could drive the car more than 35 miles an hour. If we did and Dad found out about it, we couldn't drive anymore. This rule held for some few years, but we all eventually surpassed the maximum. When a younger brother, Don, came to driving age, the threat of punishment was mostly gone. We didn't have to have licenses, but our father was equal to the law in saying who could have the car.

Our second hired man at the garage was a young fellow, also a self-trained mechanic, who owned a motorcycle. You had to be a mechanic to run one of those things. It was the kind where you pushed it down the road on the run to start it, and then hopped on as it roared away.

This fellow came back from the Kansas Free Fair at

Topeka pretty well scratched up. He had been a spectator in the motorcycle hippodrome where drivers "defied death" in spectacular rides around a circular, perpendicular wall. The spieler of the act offered $25 to any one who would attempt to do the same. Our mechanic took them on. He did all right going up, but not so good coming down. He told me he found out one thing.

"They don't go no 60 miles an hour around that wall like they say," he confided. "Twenty-five miles would be more like it."

One Saturday afternoon, our young man mechanic was attempting to start a Model T Ford which a farmer had parked in front of the old livery barn. The farmer wanted to go home and the thing wouldn't budge. The mechanic was fooling with the coil while I turned the crank for him. Obviously something was out of time because the engine was backfiring. I knew how to grip the crank handle so that if it kicked, presumably, it wouldn't crack my wrist. But this one kicked harder. The crank flew out of my hand and whirled around, catching my arm on the back side, breaking it like a stick.

Although we didn't know it at the time, this ended my career as a mechanic. Dad was getting tired of the garage anyway. He didn't mind working from 7 a. m. to 6 p. m. seven days a week in the blacksmith shop, but rebelled at the idea of fixing cars or selling gasoline at all hours of the night. So in a few months he sold the place.

Also, at the time, since I could do no mechanical work with one arm in a sling, I appealed to a relative in

Kansas City who gave me a job as an office boy on a paper called *The Kansas City Star*. I had to fib a little as to age, because the man who hired me, the late Percy Smith, said I was supposed to be 16. I worked the remainder of the summer until school started. It gave me some ideas.

There were still a few more years in Maple Hill in school, in the blacksmith shop and working on farms, but times were changing fast. My father realized the years of blacksmith shops were limited, and he had sold the garage. So, when the opportunity offered, I hung my leather apron on a nail at the shop, caught the train to Kansas City and the next day had one of *The Star's* white pencils in my pocket. I was a reporter, perhaps because of that Ford that broke my arm.

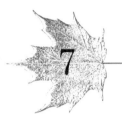

"Free Air"

Looking back over the years of development of the motor car and related industries, it is my conclusion that the most appealing sign that ever hung over a filling station said, "FREE AIR."

For the uninitiated, a hasty explanation is that prior to the free air signs, air didn't cost money. It was always free but, brother, you earned it.

Free air meant that a filling station was equipped with an air pressure tank and that you could fill your tires from an air hose—just as today. Before that there was only one way—a hand pump.

The filling stations in my home town were not the first to announce free air. I know, because I worked in one of them.

When on Saturday nights in Maple Hill, the Model T's, Overlands, Studebakers, Auburns, Chevrolets, and others began to outnumber the buggies and wagons lined up at the hitching posts on Main Street, my father started worrying about the future of the blacksmith shop.

A few tractors here and there on farms also made him wonder what to plan for me. Up to that time we'd always assumed I would learn the blacksmith trade and join him in the shop, just as he had done with his father.

But what was the future for shoeing horses, setting wagon and buggy tires and other traditional blacksmith jobs, if people were going to quit the horse and take to the car?

So, when a garage next door to the blacksmith shop was for sale, my father bought it. He went to Kansas City for a mechanic's course at Rahe's Auto School and thereafter for awhile ran both garage and the shop. My apprenticeship shifted back and forth.

The garage had a gasoline pump out front with a glass container that held 10 gallons. You turned a crank to pump gasoline from an underground tank into the glass container. Gallonage marks on the glass let you know how much gasoline you were putting into the car.

This was easy.

But it was real work when you had to pump up a tire. Fortunately, motorists didn't commonly drive up to the filling station expecting an attendant to check each tire for pressure and then pump them up to the proper level.

Virtually every car owner had his own gauge. He assumed it was his own responsibility to keep the tire properly inflated. He'd get out the old tire pump before he left home, in fact before he had cleaned up and put on his clean shirt, to make sure the tires were plentifully supplied with air.

But with a flat tire it was different. The garage fixed flats—50 cents for taking a tire off, putting a patch on a tube, putting the tire back on and pumping it up. Blowout patches for holes in the casings were extra.

There were two kinds of tires—the cincher type and those made for demountable rims. A demountable rim was a devilish device.

It was a steel rim broken in the middle so that it could be squeezed together just enough to get it into the perimeter of the tire. Then you had to spring the rim back to its original circumference so that it held tightly against the tire. This could be done with the aid of a hammer, big screw driver, and a couple of levers made from broken car springs—plus a lot of muscle power.

The clincher tires were for the small cars such as the Model T's and as the name implied, they clinched themselves to the rim. It was just a matter of stretching the casing over the rim.

This could be done also with the aid of levers made from old car springs and screw drivers along with some well-chosen words. All cars carried such equipment in a tool box under the seat—except for the well chosen words.

After the tire was mounted came the chore of pumping it up. There were single barrel pumps, double barrel pumps and my father finally bought a pump which had an air cylinder lying horizontally on a platform and you pushed a handle back and forth to force the air into the tire. This was a deluxe model but still muscle powered.

Tires carried 60, 65 and 70 pounds of air. Starting with a flat, a fellow could almost make the smoke fly as he went up and down on the hand pump or back and forth on the deluxe gadget. But you were ready to stop for a breath of air yourself when you had the pressure up to about 40 pounds. Around 60, the going got tough.

It was in this period that I learned never to put a patched tube back in a tire until the tube had been inflated and tested thoroughly in a tub of water. If there was anything discouraging, it was to go to all the work of putting a tire back on the rim, getting it pumped up and then hear the mournful sound of escaping air. It meant you had to do the whole job over again.

A stranger in a Cadillac drove into the garage one summer day with a rear tire that was losing air rapidly. I took off the tire, pulled a nail from the casing and then patched the tube. But I had an awful time getting the casing back on the demountable rim.

The Cadillac owner, growing impatient, acidly remarked that it would help if I knew what I was doing.

And I, about 14 at the time, told him I knew what I was doing all right, but the dang thing just wouldn't spring together. Actually, I may not have been experienced on that particular type of rim, but I knew that more strength than knowledge was what it took to put a tire on a rim.

I finally got the tire on, pumped up to 70 pounds,

and sent him on his way. To this day, I'd like to see him standing beside a car with a flat tire on a lonely road—I'd ride right on by.

We sold tires in our garage guaranteed to go 3,000 miles, or deluxe brands guaranteed to go 5,000. People bragged if they went to Topeka and back, 28 miles, (only 20 now) with the same air with which they started.

It was in Topeka that we saw our first "free air" sign. With elation my father stopped the car and we got our tire gauge from under the seat on our Overland to give the tires a test. Fortunately, they needed a little air so we had the opportunity to experiment with the new device.

My father got the air hose and pressed it down on the valve stem of the left front tire as my brothers and I watched. We could see the air tightening the casing. Such ease!

After a moment, my father disconnected the thing, gave the tire a kick and put on his pressure gauge.

She measured past 80 pounds!

"Stand back," he warned us, as he frantically pressed the valve to let air out. "You got to watch these things."

Motor cars didn't carry a spare in those days. In fact, usually under the seat you'd find an extra tube, patching material, and inevitable pump. Sometimes, also, a blowout boot.

Free air and the extra wheel meant a new era in motoring. Some people still keep a tire pump in the home garage, sort of a relic of the days when air in the tire was something to be appreciated. They're also good for pumping up basketballs and footballs.

As for our garage at Maple Hill, we found out that it was a 24-hour-a-day job. My father didn't like that. He insisted that 10 hours of hard work each day was enough for any man, so he sold it.

The new owner put in "free air" when electricity finally reached our town. It wasn't long until air pressure was such a common thing at filling stations that the "free air" signs disappeared.

8 Cars "Fully Stripped"

Today's modern car is advertised as "fully equipped" which means everything from air conditioning to powered windows.

Advertisements in the 1920s didn't say so, but by comparison the cars of that day could have been described as "fully stripped," particularly the less costly variety.

In fact, the motorist of the '20s and before almost started from scratch when it came to equipment. But actually it was a lot of fun adding the gadgets that later became a common part and parcel of every motor vehicle.

The Model T lent itself best to the addition of gadgets. Henry Ford believed in selling a car that boasted only the basic fundamentals.

This writer's most proud possession was a 1927 Model T coupe with wire wheels, balloon tires, a bumper in front, canvas awnings on the windows, a silver ball on the radiator cap and a Bosch ignition system. About the only thing it lacked was a speedometer and Frontenac engine head.

However, by following another car with a speedometer as a pace setter, my wire-wheeled wonder demonstrated it could do 45 miles an hour, if the road was slightly down hill.

A previous 1922 Model T couldn't be pushed beyond the 40-mile mark.

It may come as a surprise to the present hot rod generation to learn that bumpers were not standard equipment. The fact is bumpers not only did not come with the Model T's, Chevrolet, the Essex or some others, but you usually bought one for the front, not both front and rear.

The motor car of the 1920s was no pioneer vehicle. It had become a common part of the American way of life. However, the final product was much more the personal choice and selection of the owner than today's "equipped" car.

Most cars were the touring models, so locking the doors was of no use. To be safe, you bought a locking device for the steering wheel. You could also buy locking door handles for the sedans and coupes as they began to get more numerous.

Although all cars had self starters, the Model T's had a crank as standard equipment and most others carried a crank under the seat which could be used to augment the starter—when it wouldn't work. There was an anti-kicking device which you could attach on the Model T. It was advertised with the claim, "No more broken arms."

An extra large steering wheel with a lock on it was a deluxe feature which could be purchased at the stores carrying auto parts. A rear view mirror was another gadget that came into being with the glass-enclosed cars.

A real handy gadget which saved a lot of climbing out of the car in the mud and during a rain was a windshield wiper, which was worked by hand. You drove with one hand and worked the wiper with the other. The deluxe model had blades on either side, wiping the rain off the outside of the windshield and the fog from the inside.

Eventually, there came a wiper that worked from the intake vacuum.

You could get more speed, the sellers claimed, if you put on an Atwater Kent ignition system which eliminated the timer on the Ford. Admittedly, the timer could be an aggravation. With the fancy ignition system, a Stromberg carburetor and a valve grind job you could have your car in the best shape possible to start the winter.

Also for the winter you gave the car's top a coating with a black rubber-like paint and you put alcohol in the radiator. The alcohol boiled out on warm days with the result that a cold wave from the weatherman created a rush to the filling stations to get a "radiator test." You added a quart to a half gallon of alcohol with every cold morning.

One way to tell if the radiator was low on water and alcohol, or both, was to buy a radiator cap which contained a thermometer. If the radiator was about to boil—not an unusual occurrence—a red line showed up on the thermometer. You could see it from the driver's seat.

Motorists could have a choice from a wide variety of radiator ornaments. A favorite was a chrome or silver ball on which was mounted an eagle. Another featured two nickle-plated wings, the wings serving as handles which could be gripped in removing the radiator cap. The plain radiator cap which came with the car was pretty dull.

Most young fellows attached a cutout to the exhaust pipe or manifold. You could feel the pulse of the car better when you could hear the distinct firing of each cylinder. The "pulse" turned out to be a roar when you had the throttle open.

Since most cars came with hand gasoline and spark levers only, you bought your foot accelerators at the auto parts store. This required cutting a hole in the floor board, but this was of no moment. You cut a hole in the floor board, too, for the heater.

The first heaters probably were the most simple gadgets attached to cars. They cost 95 cents up for Model T's. The cheapest gadget was simply a metal guard which was put around the exhaust manifold and carried hot air through a pipe to the inside of the car.

The more expensive models—such as the one I had on my Model T—had a small metal grill which fit in the floor of the car which could be opened or closed. The pipe from the exhaust carried the hot air to this grill. While theoretically you could shut off the heat from coming into the car, it could not be stopped from reaching the grill.

When the grill got red hot it could set the wood floor

board afire. But I always could stamp it out.

If you wanted a horn better than the "buzzer" type that came with the car, you could get a motor drive Klaxon.

To be real fancy, a dash light could be purchased. Also a fog light for the front of the car. A hole was cut in the dash board for the needed switches.

The Model T's and some other cars had an annoying habit, after spindle bolts of bushings began to wear, of shimmying. This meant the front wheels wobbled and the action almost would tear the steering wheel out of your hands. This could happen in the most embarrassing places, such as in heavy traffic.

The auto stores had a remedy, an anti-shimmy device, a spring contraption which slipped on the car easily.

It was possible to install a dash oil gauge, but a more simple method to measure oil was to open a little petcock on the crank case. If oil came out, there was sufficient in the engine. This required getting down under the car, but you could carry a little rod with clamp device which fit over the petcock. This made the task rather easy.

Likewise, with a wood measuring stick, you could measure the gasoline in the car's 10-gallon tank.

For brakes presumably better than those that came on the Model T's there were the kind that had drums on the rear wheels. A simple cable attached from the brake pedal to the wheel drums. If the cable broke while you were going down hill, you were in for a thrilling experience . You could throw the car into low gear and that helped.

Cantilever shock absorbers had come into being in the '20s and were extras. So did water pumps.

To carry luggage, folding racks were obtainable for attachment to the running boards.

A man went prepared, too, for trouble, in his selection of tools. Every car carried a leaf from an old car spring as a tool for taking off tires. There were the hammer, pliers, spark plug wrench, screw driver and most important of all, a good tire pump. Since one spare tire often was not enough to assure a safe trip, it was a matter of prudence to carry a package of patches for tubes, plus a lace-on boot which could be put over a blow-out hole in a casing in an emergency.

Yes sir, a "fully equipped" car in the '20s had sort of a personality—yours. The manufacturer supplied the basic vehicle. You bought the rest.

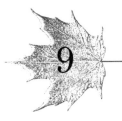

Yesterday's Sounds

9

THE mournful call of the turtle dove which I hear early in the morning through my open bedroom window of my home in Kansas City is a reminder that it is one of the few sounds still around that used to awaken my brothers and me when we slept on the front porch of our old home.

I can't remember when, for instance, I have heard a rooster crow at daybreak—in fact, I don't recall the last time I heard a rooster crow any place. Nor do I ever any more hear the hee-haw of a mule.

The fact is, many once-familiar sounds are seldom if ever heard any more, but plenty of new sounds are taking their place.

A lot of the old sounds still can be heard under certain circumstances. For instance, you can hear the whistle on the steam engine of a threshing machine when demonstrations are given at the Agricultural Hall of Fame and National Center near Bonner

Springs, Kansas. Also, there are several "threshing bees" held around the country each August where the old steam engines are fired up and the whistles blown to a fare-thee-well.

The sound may be the same during the demonstrations, but it was more thrilling when you heard the boss man give the whistle a couple of sharp toots on a hot, summer morning signaling that they were ready to have you start tossing bundles of wheat from your wagon into the separator.

But even though these sounds still are available (I guess that is the word), more and more it is true that millions of persons are born and grow to adulthood without ever hearing them.

The rooster's crow is a good example. Even relatively few farms keep laying flocks any more. Few of those that do keep roosters.

They buy "sexed" chicks; that is, they purchase only pullets which will grow into layers. Roosters still are a necessity at poultry breeding farms, but these are few in number.

Back in the days when nearly every farm had chickens and when baby chicks were raised by the old setting hen, obviously every farm had roosters. Roosters crowed to each other and apparently to the hens—crowing was about the commonest sound around the barnyard, starting early in the morning.

It used to be a cute trick for some youngsters, almost as soon as they could talk, to mimic a rooster's crow. The accomplished could make the sound as real as do those now who mimic the rattle of a machine gun or the roar of a jet plane.

We used to imagine, as we tried to keep our eyes closed against the light of the sun coming up early in the morning, that the eerie call of the turtle dove was coming from the woods down along Mill Creek.

The turtle doves always sounded far away. Actually, they were sitting in the elderberry and locust trees in our yard where they made their nests.

Our mother often expressed provocation over the slipshod way the turtle doves made their nests—just a few sticks laid across one another on which they somehow could balance an egg. However, they seemed to get the job done because the turtle dove crop thrived each year.

A sound which created a lot of pleasure for us youngsters at Maple Hill was one that came from riding on a hayrack. For our Sunday school picnics, we'd all gather at the church, where a farmer would bring his hayrack (a wagon with a large, flat bed for hauling hay) to transport us to Steele Romick's picnic grove on the banks of Mill Creek.

Few vehicles rode rougher than a hayrack. It had iron rimmed wheels and no springs. Even on good country roads there was a constant vibration and on this we cashed in by all—in chorus—making a continuous "ah-ah-ah" sound. The bounce of the hayrack gave it a staccato continuity that we thought was awfully funny.

A sound in a similar category—which must still be available someplace—was created on a picket fence. You held a stout stick against the pickets as you ran beside them. Three or four boys in a row running along a picket fence could make enough noise for anybody.

A pleasant sound that was familiar in every little town was the ring of the anvil in the blacksmith shop. It was particularly familiar to us because my father owned and operated the blacksmith shop in Maple Hill.

There are still lots on anvils around in farm machine shops and the like, but an anvil doesn't really ring unless it is on a good base. My father put his anvil on a large piece of a log.

When he hit the anvil with a hammer, the hammer bounced back. Such an anvil was "alive" and it "rang." This was the sound that you could hear blocks away from the old-time blacksmith shop. It was a pleasant sound and indicated action. When the anvil was ringing, a man was at work.

A monotonous sound few children ever hear any more is the click of the car wheels on a railroad train. Even those who ride trains have little opportunity to hear the click because rails are welded or because the passenger cars are so well insulated that the noise is eliminated.

The click could sound like a clack if you were trying to sleep. Adults used to tell us that if you could count the clicks you would hear in a minute, you could calculate the speed of the train, as the rails had a specific length. I never was that good.

For generations, a part of the rural locale was the whistle of the steam locomotive. The whistle was something you got used to if you lived along a main railroad line in the time when train traffic was heavy. Maple Hill is on the main line of the Rock Island. St. Marys, 10 miles to the north, is on the Union Pacific.

On a quiet day on the hills west of Maple Hill, you could hear the distant wail of the U. P. locomotive and compare it with that of the Rock Island. The difference in the "tune" was clear.

There was something assuring about the long toots of the late-night trains as they whistled for the main road crossing at Maple Hill. It was, when you were slightly awakened, a kind of "all-is-well" signal.

Everybody knew something was wrong when one morning around 4 o'clock a locomotive's whistle pierced the air without a break as the train sped through Maple Hill and on into the distance. The engineer could see flames that were destroying the big Tod ranch house a mile from town.

He did his best to alert the countryside and people did respond. But it was too late to save the house.

The engineer's action was an indication, however, of how the railroad men of those days felt that they were a part of the communities which they served. Many of them had acquaintances in every town.

Today's diesels carry a cluster of horns which sound the warning of approaching trains. They serve the same purpose as the whistles on the old locomotives, but somehow they haven't yet won a place in railroad lore akin to that of their predecessors. Youngsters who never have heard the wail of a steam whistle will not know the difference.

Few boys and girls in little towns—and none in cities—any longer hear the click of telegrapher's keys in the railroad stations for the simple reason that most little towns no longer have depots with regular agents.

58

The constant click of the telegraph apparatus once was as much a part of the country town depot as the coal oil lamp with its tin shade and the potbellied stove in the waiting room.

The demise of the passenger train also has stilled the voice of the conductor or head porter whose warning, "BOARD, BOARD, ALL ABOARD," told passengers that the train was about to pull out of the depot. Still recalled is the porter at the old Rock Island depot in Topeka who for one train always added, "CHANGE CARS FOR HOLTON, HORTON AND ST. JOE."

Far more people today hear the voice on the loudspeaker at the airport announce that all those boarding flight 56 for Washington should be at gate 11. But you don't even see the announcer. It could be a recording.

Another sound that has disappeared from the farm along with the crow of the rooster is the whir of the cream separator.

The cream separator was a hand-operated device that depended on whirling the milk at such a speed that the cream, being lighter than the rest of the milk, would go to the center while the skim milk circled to the outside of the vessel. The cream trickled out one little spout, while the skim milk poured out a larger one.

It was necessary to turn the crank until the apparatus reached a certain speed before a valve was turned to let the milk into the separating chamber.

Turning the crank to "wind up" the separator produced a sound similar to that on a mild siren. Youngsters had lots of fun turning the crank as long as it was play. But night and morning, Sundays included, it was a chore when the cream actually was being separated. Even worse was the washing of the separator and the milk buckets that had to follow.

Periodically, I visit farms in Missouri or Kansas where hogs are being fed. Invariably, the animals eat from automatic feeders—that is, the grain ration is automatically delivered to feeders as it is consumed. This indicates to me it no longer is common to "slop" the pigs, a procedure which produced the squealingest, slurpiest, hungriest sound imaginable.

I'm referring to the days when farmers mixed bran or shorts with skim milk or water and poured it into troughs for the pigs. No boy who ever witnessed (or listened to) the slopping of the pigs ever had any doubt what his mother meant when she scolded him at the table with the admonition, "You want people to think you eat like a hog?"

With more and more people living in cities and fewer and fewer on the farm, not many boys and girls are hearing the gutteral sound of the bullfrog.

Bullfrogs abounded in Mill Creek and in the sloughs around Maple Hill. We imagined they called to each other and we even thought we could understand what they were saying.

One big, old green frog would say in a basso profundo, "PULL HIM UNDER, PULL HIM UNDER." A hoot owl would ask, "WHO, WHO," and a big frog on the other side of the creek would answer, "SIMON-SIMON."

Well, it sounded that way.

A sound that used to be heard around schools but

60

now seems to be gone is the beat of the triangle to mark time for the orderly march of pupils from the playground back to classes following recess.

It was a privilege in our grade school at Maple Hill to get to beat the triangle. Some youngsters beat a drab BONG, BONG, BONG, BONG, BONG. Those who were more adept could almost produce syncopation: BING-BONG, BING-BONG, BING-BINGITY-BINGITY-BONG.

It might be hard to prove that clocks are any different today than they used to be, but not many years ago there weren't such things as silent electric clocks, especially out in the country.

The late Arthur Capper, as the graduation speaker for the Maple Hill High School, told a story about clocks. I think the year was 1919. He was the Kansas governor at the time.

Capper told the story to illustrate how much faster the young people were living than in an earlier day. Even courting was at a faster pace.

Why, when grandpa was a young man, Capper related, he'd sit in the parlor with his girl and the silence would be broken only by the old grandfather's clock with its pendulum swinging to and fro, seeming to say, "TAKE-YOUR-TIME, TAKE-YOUR-TIME."

Now (1919), Capper said, the little old wind-up alarm clock sits on a shelf and loudly ticks, "GIT-HER, GIT-HER, GIT-HER."

We got the point and liked the implication of being young and modern.

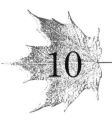

When Eating Was Fun

10

IN MY home town, when I was a youngster, we had one simple way of celebrating almost any occasion—we had a big dinner.

It didn't matter whether it was a birthday, wedding anniversary, Bobby Burns night, a farm sale, a special school or church event, lodge night.

At just any kind of a gathering, delicious food was the main item of entertainment. I use the word entertainment because we actually had a great deal of fun eating.

Of course, I was younger then and like other boys had an appetite which perhaps made all food taste good. But it was more than that. I can't recall ever hearing the word "diet" mentioned, even among the older folks.

We actually ate for the pleasure of it—and the many good cooks among the mothers of the community saw to it that we enjoyed ourselves fully.

They must have enjoyed preparing the food, even though it was all cooked on wood or coal ranges, because they vied with each other in preparing dishes that would be remembered. In fact, most of the women in town or on the farms about had specialties for which they were noted. On every occasion they brought this prize dish. Once a woman had established a reputation for a certain delicacy, there was sort of an understanding that this was to be her contribution to any community affair and she wouldn't run into competition.

Aunt Nellie kept scones in a big earthen jar in the pantry. Children who don't know what a pantry is have missed something. She also had Scotch shortbread. Aunt Nellie, along with Mrs. Billie Watt and a few other women from Scotland, made shortbread that melted in your mouth. There's no reason it shouldn't melt; the recipe starts out, "Take one cup of butter . . ."

There were many people from Scotland in Maple Hill and this led to the formation of the Scotch Birthday Club. Although started by women who had come from Scotland, the rules soon were broadened to include wives or daughters of Scots. The club met on the birthday of every member—to eat.

Lucky were the menfolks in the household which was the host, because the leftovers were more than enough for a banquet. I knew we were in for a bountiful supper (mostly desserts) when I came home from school and saw the farm wives' horses and buggies around our yard. There would be Aunt Nellie's sorrel, Old Speck; Mrs. Frank McClelland's black

Topsy, Mrs. W. J. Tod's team of sorrels, Mrs. Horace Adam's fancy black, Mrs. Jim Thompson's slick bay. The Thompsons always had beautiful horses.

With some variation, the same women who belonged to the Scotch Birthday Club also belonged to the Ladies Aid society, the Eastern Star and the Royal Neighbors. Of course, they also were the women of our church. Their husbands were the members of the Modern Woodmen and the Masons. And every organization had its dinner.

Baby-sitters apparently hadn't yet come into vogue, because the mothers of Maple Hill took their youngsters with them. As youngsters, most often we didn't get to sit at the main table, but I never heard a complaint.

It was from these dinners that I remember Mrs. McClelland's gingerbread or her steamed brown bread, cooked in coffee cans. You got a slice just the size of the coffee can and spread a layer of home-churned butter across it.

There was Mrs. Winkler's mocha cake, made, I heard them say, with two cups of butter. In fact, in later years I learned that one reason everything tasted so good was the generous use of butter and cream in a good share of the cooking.

After I had married a girl in Kansas City, I took her back to Maple Hill to introduce her to one of the big dinners. She thought Mrs. Oscar Hammarlund's chocolate cake with its thick fudge icing was the richest thing she ever had tasted. Mrs. Hammarlund (a Swede) baked her cake in a huge pan that just fitted the oven of her wood range. When she cut the cake in squares, it was almost like laying out rows for checker-planted corn in a field. Each big square of the rich chocolate was a sight to behold.

My wife wanted the recipe.

"Well, you take two cups of cream . . .," Mrs. Hammarlund began.

It was no use, my wife said later. In Kansas City, we could not afford to use cream that way. She had learned, too, that the reason a bowl of lima beans tasted so good was that it contained a cup of fresh cream.

Sometimes I think the difference between now and what some people like to refer to as the good old days is cream.

In Maple Hill, the cooks used cream on nearly everything. We had gobs of cream on the pumpkin pie, cream on the cake, whipped cream in the fruit salads, cream jello dessert. The whipped cream was served in a bowl and you took what you wanted. It wasn't squirted from a can.

Fattening? I can't recall hearing the word. Of course, people worked harder and outdoors. They needed more food for energy.

In our Scotch family, oatmeal was a standard dish for breakfast. We actually thought that if you didn't get your oatmeal each morning, likely you would not get your full growth. Once in a while my mother would order oatmeal by the sack—a gunny sack—lined with muslin of course.

In addition to oatmeal for breakfast, oatmeal cookies were a mainstay at nearly all functions. It must be obvious by now that most of the dinners we had at

Maple Hill were affairs where every family contributed part of the food.

Then there were big sugar cookies—sometimes three or four inches across.

Mrs. Tom Oliver made the best doughnuts in the world.

Mrs. Ida Carlson supplied graham cracker pie. If my memory is wrong on which woman cooked what, it is because, I must confess, I was thinking mostly of the good food.

My mother baked huge loaves of bread, using a starter that was kept "alive" year in and year out. If something happened to that starter it was a calamity.

Naturally, there were foods besides dessert. In late summer fried chicken was the special treat. The fryers were young roosters that would weigh four to five pounds. A drumstick from a chicken that size was a rather hefty serving.

When the frying chicken season was over we had a dish I never see any more. It was called pressed chicken. A rooster was cooked. The meat was taken from the bone and ground up. Mixed with other tasty ingredients, it was put into a crock, with a plate on top of it, and pressed under a brick. The chicken was served as a spread for sandwiches. Spread thickly on my mother's homemade bread, this was a wonderful meal in itself, but of course, we never stopped with just a sandwich.

We always had baked beans. I don't know how they were cooked, except I remember the women always started with white navy beans. It was a long process which began with soaking the beans. Later they were baked, covered with a layer of molasses and strips of bacon.

Then there were mashed potatoes into which butter had been whipped. Mashed potatoes and butter covered with thick chicken or beef gravy will keep you warm in cold weather.

Homemade pickles were part of every dinner. Some women brought huge sliced dills and others the tiny sweet varieties. In addition there would be pickled beets, pickled peaches and crabapples. Some cooks were known for their tasty watermelon pickles.

At a big dinner it caused no comment if you filled your plate to the brim with vegetables and meat, pickles and the like. Then when this was gone, you returned for a piece of angelfood cake, a slice of chocolate cake, a piece of lemon pie and perhaps a little jello and whipped cream on the side.

It was considered the thing to do to sample everything. In fact, you might hurt some good cook's feelings if you passed up her dish. We tried gloriously not to offend.

There were extra special occasions when the menu was diversified. For instance, once a year the Woodmen had an oyster supper. The oyster stew was cooked in a copper wash boiler on a coal oil range in the lodge hall. For this event the local stores ordered oyster crackers—the only time of the year we had them, as I recall.

Long tables made of boards on trestles were set up in the hall. You'd take your bowl to the little annex, where the wash boiler on top of the stove held the piping hot stew. With a tin cup, a member of the lodge dished it out. Crackers and pickles were on the tables.

After the oyster supper, sometimes our parents would remove the tables, scatter wax on the floor and there'd be a dance. Youngsters would sit in chairs along the walls and watch. But mostly after dinner people just visited until it was time to go home.

Bobby Burns Night was a big night at Maple Hill, too, for years. Somehow, even though Kansas had prohibition, some of the celebrants managed to get a little something to drink.

One night there was a fight and one fellow went home with the announced intention of getting his shotgun. He was going to return and settle his grievances once and for all. Some people thought maybe he would, so that ended the party. It also ended the Bobby Burns celebrations.

A gala occasion always was a farm sale. Handbills posted at the bank, the blacksmith shop, the elevator and at the grocery stores announced the date of sale, listed horses, wagons, plows and other items "too numerous to mention" which were to be sold at auction. The handbill also would state that luncheon would be served by the Ladies Aid.

The luncheon had to be home-cooked as there was no other source of food. This included the pies. You could get a piece of pie for a dime, a ham sandwich for another dime and pop or coffee for a nickel. Everybody went to the sales, whether they intended to buy or not. Likely as not they'd see something going at a bargain price and make a bid. There's something appealing about an auction—and you could always get a good lunch.

As youngsters we had fun eating even though there was no party. Maybe it was because we had so few other types of entertainment. There was no opportunity for instance, to go to a local drive-in for a hamburger and malt. You could get ice cream at the drugstore and a bowl of chili or a ham sandwich at Jim Fyfe's pool hall and lunch counter. But this never was a hangout for youngsters.

It was more fun when you were living to eat rather than eating to live.

Cow Pasture Baseball

THE aspersions cast on "cow pasture baseball" in the contract controversy with Kansas City Athletics owner, Charles O. Finley, struck me both as amusing and misleading.

It suggested there was something degrading or perhaps uninteresting about playing baseball in a pasture.

No doubt cow pasture baseball could create problems for a sophisticated Kansas City, financial and otherwise. I suppose there would be difficulties in handling the crowds, chasing home runs and parking in the mud.

But we got along just fine playing in pastures in our old home town.

Just across the road from our house in Maple Hill was Updegraff's pasture, a couple of acres or so where R. T. Updegraff, grocer and lumberman, kept a cow and a black horse which pulled his delivery wagon.

After school and in summer, this pasture was a gathering place for both boys and girls for baseball games. Home plate would be a gunny sack; first, second and third, pieces of rock or board. The bases could be spaced according to the size of the players.

Pastures had certain attributes for baseball. First and foremost was the fact horses and cows kept the grass clipped close to the ground, making an ideal place to play. There was unlimited room, with no nearby windows to break.

There were also some disadvantages, as those with experience will recall; but these didn't present too much difficulty if you kept your eyes open. You could get quite a surprise if you were on a dead run for a fly ball and neglected to look down as well as up.

The Maple Hill school yard had all kinds of room for baseball. First there was the immediate playground adjacent to the school. Then "across the ditch," a big ravine that divided the several acres of school property, was a pasture-like field with adequate space for baseball, football or track. In the days when the local rural route mail carriers used horses, they got free pasturage on the school land.

It was on this school property that the town's baseball field was established. In the spring, some farmer would donate the use of a team and mower, and clip the grass and weeds in the baseball area. Then four horses would be hitched on the township road drag and the infield would get a going-over. Bags of sand made the bases.

Here the school and the town teams played. Of course we didn't have grandstands that would seat

30,000 people—in fact we didn't have any at all. Neither was there a board fence around the field. For a backstop we had four posts with chicken wire stretched between them.

But don't think these inadequacies interfered with the excitement of the game. In fact, spectators were a lot closer to the players than those who sit in the major league grandstands. The more cautious, such as women with children, watched from behind the wire backstop; but most of the men and boys found places along the sidelines between home and first, or home and third.

This put you in much closer contact not only with the players, but the umpire. Umpires in our games always stood behind the pitcher, not the catcher, and the one official not only called strikes and balls but made all decisions on the bases.

In a big league game players or the coaches can get riled at the umpire's decisions, can shake their fingers under an umpire's nose and they can also, if the umpire so rules, be banished from the park simply with a wave of the official's hand. Spectators may merely shout from their points of vantage hundreds of feet from the umpire, or perhaps throw a harmless pop bottle onto the field.

But in pasture baseball it was different. A spectator on the sidelines could shout directly at the umpire and if he became sufficiently disturbed, could walk out on the field for personal insults. In cases where a man just no longer could stand the terrible judgment of the umpire, he could pick up a ball bat and go out on the field for a definite settlement of the matters at hand.

This action, obviously, put the umpire on the defensive and also all those on the sidelines who were favoring his decisions. This could bring more ball bats into the fray and you could end the ball game right there unless cooler heads immediately prevailed.

It was just such situations as the one described that caused my mother when I was a small boy to turn thumbs down on attendance at Sunday afternoon games. She insisted the carryings on were a disgrace and couldn't see why grown men were not able to play ball without a fight. Her trouble was that she didn't realize how you could get into the spirit of the game when you were there on the sidelines.

As I recall, the "saner heads" did eventually prevail and a few of the more enthusiastic spectators were cautioned to stand back or there just wouldn't be any more ball at Maple Hill. But that didn't mean you couldn't cheer the players.

Paxico, a community about 10 miles to the west, was known as a town which did its best to get the goat of the opposing pitcher. People used to go to the games to see how Paxico's rooting section operated along the sidelines. It was a time for wholesale wisecracks, and the going was better if the pitcher was a hired specialist, say from a big town like Topeka.

"Your mama know you're out, little Topeka boy?" somebody would call. "Better watch out, that man goin' to hit that ball clear through you."

Such spontaneous humor would bring belly laughs all up and down the base lines and the hecklers would be encouraged to loosen all their inhibitions. It would get real noisy.

The pitcher, the only stranger in the entire assemblage, would calmly ignore the crowd, and suggest by his action his superiority over the common run of amateur players on the field. I do recall, however, that sometimes the tormenting was effective and it was a great time for everyone when it became obvious that the visiting specialist ($5 a game) had to be replaced by a local hurler.

Games were played in those days with a $1.25 ball. There were baseballs of various kinds, but the best and those used in real games simply were known as $1.25 balls. Every boy longed to own one, but few ever did. In our high school games and in the town team contests, each team supplied one good ball.

In the cow pasture games or those played on what we used as regular playing fields, small boys got the jobs of being "pig tail" and scurried after it. The game wouldn't proceed until it was recovered.

With no board fence around the field, a home run was a ball hit so far that the fielder couldn't get it back to home plate in time to catch the runner. Sometimes a homer would be hit so far out into the field that it would land in high grass beyond the area which had been mowed. A subsequent foul ball into the weeds back of the backstop at the same time could halt the game until one or the other of the balls was found.

When diligent searching failed to turn up the lost ball, a time-honored method was used by us boys to indicate about where it was certain to be lying. You put some saliva in the palm of one hand and then hit it smartly with the forefinger of the other hand. By some magic the "spit" would fly in the direction of the hidden ball. This didn't always work for every individual; but if enough boys tried it, eventually one would make a lucky shot and the ball would be discovered.

We played cow pasture baseball when a bunch of boys could gather at some farm on a Sunday afternoon. The country schools would have baseball games on the last day of the eight-month terms. District 83, a one-room school near Maple Hill, always celebrated the last day of school with a big basket dinner and a baseball game in which pupils, visitors and the farmer dads engaged.

The playing field was a 160-acre pasture adjacent to the school. Of course we didn't use all 160 acres, just whatever it took.

So let's not be sarcastic about pasture baseball. It has its place and it has entertained thousands, yes even millions of people across rural America.

Incidentally, the baseball field at Maple Hill now has a tiny grandstand, a building which serves as a concession stand and most important of all, lights for night games. In fact, its baseball facilities compare with those in Kansas City if you consider that Maple Hill has about 275 people while Greater Kansas City has more than a million. Not only that, Maple Hill has had no rows over contracts.

One more thing. Since I have been writing these stories about the old home town, many people have wondered where is Maple Hill. It seems to me anybody should know where Maple Hill is; but to be specific it is about 100 miles west of Kansas City and about 20 miles west of Topeka and two miles north of I-70 highway.

Thrills and Terror
When Fire Struck Town

THE most terrifying sound in all the world to those of us who lived in Maple Hill was the cry of "fire" in the middle of the night. It meant somebody's home, somebody's grocery store or other business was burning down, despite everything we could do and the truth is, we did everythmg we could to put out the fire.

The trouble was, little towns like Maple Hill just didn't have the facilities to fight a fire. A bucket brigade or a chemical apparatus were pitifully inadequate when a blaze was roaring through a roof or smoke pouring out of all the windows.

Things are different now, or at least I thought they were. The town has a water system, fire hydrants and a fire truck. There is even a siren that is supposed to alert everybody and bring the volunteers to man the firefighting equipment.

But a fire apparently still can be a shocking experience in Maple Hill. Word from my old home town about a recent fire came in the form of the minister's message in the Maple Hill Community Church weekly bulletin.

The Rev. James A. Christopher wrote:

"Last Saturday many of us in Maple Hill shared in the unpleasant task of helping put out a fire. When the Holmes family sat down to lunch that day, they had no idea what evening would find them doing. We don't go around expecting our house to catch on fire, and when it happens, we have to act quickly.

"People did act fast. The fire trucks were at the scene in about two minutes or less. Men and women came from all over town to help. Boys in high school were in there pitching with everyone else. There was little evidence of lack of desire and willingness to help, and every bit of help was necessary and appreciated.

"What was alarming to me, however, was the obvious lack of knowledge and skill on the part of just about everyone when it came to operating the fire equipment. If the wind had been blowing, three minutes would have been a long time to stop and figure out which end of the hose hooks up to the fire plug. Or if the temperature had been a little colder and the water were freezing, there wouldn't have been a chance to experiment with how many people a ladder will hold, and how many men need to hold the hose and that sort of thing.

"If the fire had been larger and more damaging, we couldn't possibly have taken orders from the dozen or so who were trying to help give directions on what was happening and what needed to be done.

"What if someone were caught inside? Would we know how to get them out? We can repair houses, but burned arms rarely come out looking like new.

"If we need to take time to learn some things that should become second nature in face of emergencies, then let's take time. If we need to spend some money to get the equipment we need to properly guard against fires, then let's spend it. That siren cannot be heard by half the people in Maple Hill. Can't we do something about that?

"Unfortunately, there likely will be a next time. I hope it does not find us as unprepared as the last few times have."

The admonition dished out by the minister to his church members should be heeded by them and by all little towns—even though it doesn't seem to be accompanied by a Biblical text. Doubtless the pastor was rather frustrated by his experience in helping to put out a fire.

He was right, of course. But he is a young man and doubtless will find that unless he can keep the people of Maple Hill interested in periodical test runs with the fire department, there'll come another day, just as he predicted, perhaps two or three years from now, when new and excited hands will, without experience, be frantically and inefficiently attempting to fight a fire.

I know from experience that Maple Hill was "practicing" fighting fires as long as 50 years ago, and our town had reason because fires came with unhappy regularity. A difference between then and now is that apparently they are able now occasionally to put out the fire before the whole building burns down. Mr. Christopher in his editorial spoke of "Helping to put out the fire" and later commented that "if the fire had been larger and more damaging," there would have been less time for mistakes.

When I was a boy, we rarely were successful in putting out the fire. The building burned to the ground and this was the case in most fires either in town or on the farm. When you drive down the highway and see a chimney standing amid ash covered ruins surrounded by a few trees in a farmstead, you realize how complete the tragedy has been, that was the way it was most of the time.

My first recollection of Maple Hill's fire department is of a light wagon, built in the shop Tom Oliver had in connection with my father's blacksmith shop.

The wagon carried four lengths of ladders and hanging on each side on iron hooks was a row of galvanized buckets. The word "fire" had been painted in red on each bucket.

This wagon, which could be pulled either by horses or men, was housed in the livery stable, a rambling big red building just south of our blacksmith shop. The livery stable was open all night—that is somebody always slept on a couch in the office.

Obviously, this fire equipment served only two purposes. It supplied a ready source of buckets and ladders. These buckets were in addition to those which all "fire fighters" attempted to bring with them. When you heard that terrible cry of fire in the night, you slipped on shoes and trousers, grabbed the water bucket in your home and ran to the scene of the blaze.

The women folks followed soon after and they helped, too. When the fire was downtown—where most of them were—there was the town well in the middle of the street at the town's main intersection, the well at the blacksmith shop, the cistern behind Jim Fyfe's restaurant and pool hall, and a few wells at homes nearby.

Men, boys and women formed a bucket line, with some man vigorously working the pump handle seeking to keep a steady stream of water pouring from the well. Buckets of water were moved hand to hand until they reached the men on the ladders and on the roof.

As the minister said of the recent fire, people worked hard. In fact, they worked their hearts out. There was shouting, weeping, confusion and even heroism, but most of the time to no avail. The well or cistern would go dry. Or we just couldn't get the water fast enough.

I was still a very small boy when the town invested in a new fire engine. This was a 2-wheeled cart with a 120-gallon water tank. In connection with the tank there was a small compartment which held, as I recall, a bottle of some kind of acid. When there was a fire alarm, the first man to the machine pulled a lever which broke the bottle and, as the cart was pulled to the fire, this was mixed with the water. By the time you got to the fire, pressure had built up in the tank and the water could be directed on the fire through a hose which was carried in a big reel on the apparatus.

Mr. Christopher may be interested to know we had a practice run at the time this new equipment was purchased. The demonstration, put on by the salesman who sold the town fathers on the machine, was well advertised for a summer's night.

The small boys in town helped the men that day prepare for the demonstration by carrying all the wood boxes and old lumber that could be found to form a huge pile on an isolated part of the school grounds.

That night we all gathered on Main Street near the town garage where the fire engine was housed. It was a festive occasion, despite the fact the people of Maple Hill were well aware of the tragedy of fire.

Somebody was sent to set fire to the big pile of boxes. Then, at a signal, men grabbed the long handle of the fire engine and started to the scene as fast as they could pull the vehicle. We boys and the women and girls ran along.

The "expert" showed the men of the town how to direct the stream from the hose to the base of the fire, not to waste it on the flame and smoke up above. It was good advice and it worked in putting out the box fire.

The trouble was, as the townsmen later were to learn, that it was difficult to get at the base of the fire in a basement, attic or back room to which you couldn't force access. You ended up pouring the water on the blaze wherever you could see it.

Maple Hill's main business block (on one side of the street) was once a series of wood buildings, with one or two exceptions. In fact, once there had been a wood sidewalk, but that was replaced by concrete.

One by one these buildings burned. There was the

pool hall, the grocery stores, the doctor's offices, the hardware store. People "talked." No one ever knew how these fires started and there was suspicion that perhaps robbers broke into the places and sought to cover their crimes by burning the buildings. Some people even suggested quietly that Rufe King, the town's bad man, who later died in the penitentiary, might have started the blazes. But Rufe, because of his reputation (somewhat apparently deserved), undoubtedly got accused of many things he didn't do. Rufe was among the bravest fire fighters of all. After he was in prison for murder, his fire fighting bravado was discussed both pro and con in connection with the series of Maple Hill fires.

Newspaper men on the *Capital* and *Journal* at Topeka used to say that whenever there was a dull night, they always could depend on a fire at Maple Hill for a story. But that was long ago.

The mornings after the fires, people would walk down Main Street to look at the ruins. We boys would take sticks and stir the ashes below the spot where the money drawer had been in the stores and sometimes find pennies or nickels. Men would talk about what they had done wrong—or right—in fighting the blaze. And everybody wondered—what caused it?

Those were days, of course, when all heating was by coal stoves and lights were coal oil lamps. These usually were the sources of fires in homes and people would know this because they would be at home at the time the blaze started. But the fires that broke out in the middle of the night downtown remained mysteries.

There are no wood buildings on Maple Hill's Main Street now for the reason the city council long ago passed an ordinance that only buildings of brick or stone could be erected there.

Eventually our family had a personal interest in the fire department as my father bought the garage where the fire engine was housed. By this time, the town had purchased a red fire cart with a bigger tank. It was supposed to be better than the initial one. For one thing, it had a coil of rope which could be extended from the front permitting a large group of men to pull the apparatus, if they were available.

Here, again, there were troubles. Not always were the men available on time.

The central office sounded the general alarm one snowy evening, consisting of five or six consecutive rings on the telephone. Everybody knew this meant trouble. The only other ways to warn of a fire were for the people to run from their houses screaming "fire," or for someone to ring the bell on the old Methodist Church.

This night the fire was in the flue of a small home at the north end of town, a long pull for a hand-drawn cart.

Several men and boys arrived at the garage to get the fire machine. My brother, Bernard, and I, were among the first because our father had directed us to run ahead with the keys.

We pulled the cart from the garage and headed into the snow for the scene of the fire. But we had difficulties the experts never had mentioned. There were drifts on the road and we didn't have the manpower to pull through them. Finally we abandoned the apparatus and ran on to the fire to see what help we could give. Fortunately the people living in the house had managed to squelch the blaze themselves. It hadn't amounted to much. A good thing.

Without the fire machine we could have, if necessary, done what we did at most fires, and that was to carry out anything in the house that was loose and set it in the yard. In actuality, in most cases this salvage was our greatest accomplishment.

It was while we still owned the garage that one night Bernard and I were awakened by bright light shining in our upstairs bedroom window. This had to be fire, of course, because there were no lights in the town, Bernard looked out the window and yelled "Fire."

In our block, one of the town's largest houses, the Doc Silverthorne home, was on fire. Flames already were coming through the roof. The Silverthornes no longer lived there and it was occupied by a new doctor and his family, Dr. King. They were away from home for the night.

Bernard and I grabbed our overalls, got the keys and headed for the garage. My mother alerted the central office and Mrs. Mabel Clark, the telephone operator, sounded the alarm.

Bernard and I were running down the street when we heard R. T. Updegraff coming out of his home screaming "Fi-re—Fi-re." The Updegraffs once had lost a beautiful home and the family barely escaped. R. T., with a huge booming voice, could put more chill into his cry of fire than anyone else in town. Old timers still remember it.

At the garage we were met by Jim Hutchins, the mechanic who worked for my father. He already had the door open. Three of us pulled the fire cart into the street. One more man joined us, but we had gone nearly a block before others arrived. By that time we were played out. Others did arrive soon, but by the time we got to the fire it was no use. Only a little furniture was salvaged.

My last time to see a fire in Maple Hill was after I had started to work for *The Star* and had gone home one Saturday evening to visit my parents. When I got there the people of the town were all at a small home where a blaze had started in the kitchen. Fortunately, this time the volunteers had been able to get to the fire on time and had put the water at the base of the blaze. They had even cut a hole in the roof so that the water could be put directly on the fire.

As I was watching the final moments of this successful accomplishment, one of the men of the town who had arrived too late to help walked into the house and stood in the kitchen looking up through the hole in the ceiling.

A fire fighter standing on the roof with a bucket of water in his hands couldn't resist the temptation. He emptied the bucket.

This was the only time I ever saw anything humorous about a Maple Hill fire.

Barefoot 'n Fancy Free

PERHAPS one thing that hasn't changed since I was a boy is the joyous excitement created by the last day of school. At least I would guess (and hope) that youngsters today are just as happy at that time of the year as I and other boys and girls were in Maple Hill some 50 years ago. Our school always "let out" around May 20 to 25.

We really didn't dislike school as much as our jubilation over the last day would indicate. In fact, even though we wouldn't admit it, we were glad to see school take up again the first Monday in September, when our fall term always started. We'd never heard of Labor Day.

The thrill of the last day of school was that we would be free, or virtually so, of all obligations for the whole summer. You HAD to go to school. But in summer, a Maple Hill boy didn't actually HAVE to do anything.

Of course there was work to do. But it didn't come every day, like school.

Thus it was that our emotions were high on that last Friday when we went to school just to get our report cards. Everybody knew there'd be no lessons. Why, we'd be out before noon—just like a holiday all in itself. The teachers would be all smiles because they, too, were free to go home.

Our teachers nearly always were Kansas girls, except for the man who was principal of the high school. The young women "roomed" at one of the homes in town large enough to have an extra bedroom. During the summer, they'd always go home or to Emporia for another session at the State Normal College. We wouldn't see them again until fall. Actually, most of them taught only a few years until they got married. Some of them married the young men who had grown up on Maple Hill farms. It was considered something special for a young man about town to "date" one of the school teachers. It always "caused talk," but not entirely adverse.

We usually had three grade school teachers and three in the high school, including the principal.

We youngsters didn't care about the teacher's social life. In reality, we considered them old women, even if they were only 20 or 21. But there was no animosity on the last day of school. We were sincere in our good-bys and they with theirs.

One freedom that came with the last day of school was the custom of going barefoot. In our day there was no rule that you had to wear shoes to school and many of us boys didn't if May was a warm month. And we could go barefoot again in September, but that had its disadvantages. During the summer the school playgrounds would grow high with weeds. In late August the school board would hire a farmer with horses and a mowing machine to cut the weeds and this would leave a multitude of sharp stubbles that were terrible on bare feet until the stubbles all had been worn down.

But in summer you could go barefoot all the time, except for one hour on Sunday morning. Even then, although our mother didn't like it, she'd occasionally let my brothers and me go barefoot to Sunday School if it avoided a big argument and if we washed our feet.

"Seems as if you'd be willing to put your shoes on for one hour and look halfway decent," she'd admonish us. Our father would acquiesce, but we knew he wasn't going to Sunday School. He always went to the blacksmith shop early Sunday morning to do his week's bookwork. He did, however, go to church.

May and June were months when the catfish bit best in Mill Creek. The bullheads were biggest and fattest in the slough along the railroad tracks also in early summer. You always could get long, fat earthworms in the moist soil near the slough. And we could catch minnows with our nets made from gunny sacks fastened to willow poles. We seined the gravel-bottomed riffles in Mill Creek for the minnows which we used to bait our trot lines.

Setting trot lines was one of the best things of the summer. It was like everything else—you didn't do it every day, but you did go fishing when you wanted to. Some days, you didn't want to do anything and that was all right, too.

Mill Creek ran fast and clean in May and June. We could seine a batch of minnows, bait our trot lines and then go swimming.

We boys slept on the porch in the summer. It was fun to wake up at daylight to the singing of the red birds, robins and wrens and the cooing of the turtle doves.

We'd get up from our cots, slip on our overalls and head down the dirt road to the creek a mile or so away. We could be back by the time our father was heading for the blacksmith shop. He always opened the shop promptly at 7 a.m. and shut the doors just as promptly at 6 in the evening.

Seldom a day went by that we didn't spend part of it at the shop. When we were small, we'd fill our pockets with rivets lying on the floor under the vise at the work bench where they had fallen as they were knocked from mowing machine section knives. New rivets always were used when my father put new section knives in the sickle bars. The old rivets, heavy little pieces of soft iron about as big as the lead in a .22 rifle cartridge, made excellent ammunition for a slingshot—better than rocks.

Our slingshots were made of strips of rubber from old inner tubes tied to a forked prong cut from a tree. We'd spend hour after hour walking along country roads shooting at blackbirds and spatsies (sparrows), sitting on telephone and fence wires. The odds must have been heavily with the birds, because we seldom if ever hit one.

I must confess, however, that we tried. Any sympathy for birds had not developed at that age.

An unsurpassed time of the summer was in the evening. Perhaps the greatest pleasure of all was to get in the car, with the top down, and ride around the countryside on freshly dragged roads.

Fourth of July started at least two weeks before the holiday and since restrictions on the sale of fireworks were very liberal, if existent at all, we were inhibited only by the number of nickels and pennies we could garner for the purchase of caps and firecrackers.

We made our own cannons out of gallon syrup buckets with carbide from carbide lamps for the explosive power. You punched a nail hole in the bottom of the bucket. Then, after putting a small hunk of carbide in the bucket along with a few drops of water, you pressed the lid on tightly. One foot was held over the bucket and one finger placed over the hole in the bottom. When gas inside built up to where it felt warm on the finger, you touch a match to the hole. There'd be a tremendous explosion which would blow the bucket lid 20 feet.

I still don't know whether this was "safe and sane," but it sure was loud and cost hardly anything at all.

Our father believed in celebrating on the Fourth so we always had a generous supply of firecrackers, Roman candles, sky rockets, pinwheels and the like, along with fried chicken and a freezer of ice cream.

This was living. No wonder we liked the summer vacation.

As mentioned earlier, we also worked in the summer. Our first work for pay came at age 9 or 10 when we were employed by ranchers and farmers in the harvest of alfalfa hay. The first job was to ride the horse that pulled the hay fork lifting hay from hayracks into the big hay barns. The pay was $1 a day or in reality, 10 cents an hour. You got the dollar if you could get in 10 hours work. If the dew was heavy and the alfalfa couldn't be handled until dried by the sun, you might get in only 8 hours, which meant just 80 cents pay.

As you grew a little older and became more experienced with horses, you were promoted to driving the teams to the hayracks as they pulled hayloaders across the broad alfalfa fields. The ultimate in seniority for a boy came when he was allowed to have his own team and operate either a side delivery or a dump rake. My first team was made up of two huge mules, Pete and Maude. The only way I could get the bridles on them was to stand in the feedbox in their stalls. Otherwise, I couldn't reach over their ears.

Nobody was ever more proud than I when I held the lines on this team of mules as I joined with the other "men" in the haying crew at the start of a morning's work—even though the pay still was only $1 a day.

We boys also were hired in the wheat harvest to shock the bundles of grain and as we grew even older, we ran the bundle wagons for the threshing machines. By this time, not only did we get higher pay, but we preferred a wage to an idle day. The wheat harvest was more exciting than putting up hay. Crews were bigger, the days longer and the dinners better. It was hot, dusty, dirty work, but it was all "volunteer." You not only didn't have to do it—like going to school—but you appreciated the money. Not only that, you were called a hired "man."

Then there was cherry-picking time. We picked cherries at home and in Frank Adams's orchard.

The pay was 10 cents a gallon and in a good day, you could make your dollar.

We had a big yard to mow with a hand mower and the garden to hoe. There also was one very difficult job that came once each summer—washing the windows in the blacksmith shop. While our father ordinarily didn't remunerate us for work at home, he would pay 10 cents a window at the shop. The trouble was the windows got awfully dirty and Dad insisted on them being cleaned thoroughly. That was his way. A job had to be done completely and right. He inspected every window before he paid the dime and if as much as one fly speck still showed, you had to wash some more.

We helped, too, with other chores at home. In fact, nearly every day we managed to get in some work, but it wasn't steady, as in school. Except for the days we were working on farms or ranches, we always could find the time at some hour to go swimming, fishing, play baseball or anything that came to mind. But as the days got hotter and drier and the dog days of August set in, even summer began to pall. Oh, of course, there was the Kaw Valley farmer who came to town two or three times a week with his wagonload of red ripe watermelons. And there was the annual August Sunday School picnic.

Mill Creek became sluggish. We didn't fish in August.

So, what the heck. We wouldn't publicize the fact, but we did rather look forward to the first Monday in September.

Nature's
Cooling Breezes

14

WHEN I was a boy the word "patio," as far as we were concerned, wasn't in the dictionary. Air conditioning hadn't been invented and it wouldn't have made any difference if it had, because we didn't have electricity.

So, come the hot summer days, we didn't get out the patio furniture, the chaise lounges, the wrought iron tables with the big umbrellas, the redwood tables and benches, or the barbecue grills. Nor did we turn on the air conditioner or the electric fans.

But we did have our own brands of summer appurtenances which sufficed for their day and helped us to enjoy shade and the evening breezes.

The deluxe item in the summer furniture category was the lawn swing. This was a two-seated affair, the seats facing each other, and with a platform for your feet in the middle. The whole thing hung in a frame. In the evening up to four people could sit on the seats and swing gently back and forth, while they visited and enjoyed available breezes.

We had one of the swings in our big yard and so did the Weavers. Ours even played a romantic role. My mother's pretty niece, Ethel Butler, then of Everest, Kansas, and now of Denver, visited us frequently in the summer, and just as frequently a caller was Sam Wiley, a young bookkeeper at one of Maple Hill's big ranches.

The situation created an ideal arrangement for my brother, Bernard, and me. Sam, glad to get rid of us, let us ride his horse, with me in the saddle and Bernard behind, while he and Ethel sat in the lawn swing.

Everything must have worked out well, because Sam and Ethel married.

The most common summer convenience was the porch swing. Almost every family had one. Even those who didn't have porches would hang one of the swings from a big tree limb or between two trees in the yard. Most of the swings would seat two or three people but the super deluxe model would be 6 feet long and a person could lie down on it.

The ideal location for a porch swing was on a screened-in porch with a south exposure. Unfortunately, not every home afforded the luxury of a porch that was screened.

Summer furniture had to be in the shade with full access to the breezes, protected as far as possible from flies and mosquitoes, and, in general, of a nature that wouldn't be soiled by working clothes. The latter was a practical point. Most people in Maple Hill, and certainly all the farmers, did manual work.

At noontime, in particular, when a man had a chance for a 10- or 15-minute nap before going back to a hot, sweaty job, he appreciated a place where he could lie down in his work clothes. This was one reason why so many homes had an old leather couch on the porch—a couch that had lost its place of prominence in the parlor, but was ideal as outdoor summer furniture. Farmers, after doing the evening chores, which nearly always included milking the cows, didn't change from overalls to a summer linen suit.

We also had a homemade hammock made of barrel staves. The staves were held together with wires woven over and under each of the pieces of wood and the wires then were twisted together at the end to make a "rope" to be tied to a tree.

Barrel-stave hammocks probably were not the most comfortable places for a rest, but they did provide air circulation and you never had to take them in out of the rain. They could be made a little more comfortable if you spread on old quilt on them.

Hammocks made of cloth, with fringed edges and pillows, were quite popular and a little on the elite side. People used to say that a girl sitting in a hammock with a young man was perfectly safe. If at first you don't believe that, think about it.

A few people had wooden lawn chairs which had been made from patterns which appeared in the old *Weekly Kansas City Star*. But for the most part, we sat in chairs that no longer were good enough to be used inside the house. There'd be an old rocker or two, which you could move around the yard to keep pace with shade under the biggest maple tree. Nearly always, too, on farms, there'd be the bench that was used to hold wash basins for the men as they cleaned up at noon and at night.

Untold hours of summer comfort were provided in front of the garage and a store or two in downtown Maple Hill by leather seats salvaged from the old-time touring cars. Elderly men, who spent a good part of the hot summer days loafing, found the car seats adequate, if not luxurious. The old boys sat in the shade on the east side of Main Street in the morning and moved to the west side in the afternoon.

As far as I can recall, we never once had a carton or case of pop at our house. And neither did anyone else. It just wasn't the common thing to do, particularly because so few people had ice. So, consequently, on a summer's evening while we were sitting in our porch swing or on the old chairs on the lawn, we would not serve cold drinks.

We could, of course, go downtown to either the drugstore or Jim Fyfe's restaurant and pool hall and buy bottles of strawberry, lemon, raspberry or cream pop. We drank them where we bought them, while they were cold. Occasionally, we could splurge with a malted milk with nutmeg sprinkled on top.

Sitting in our yard at Maple Hill on a clear summer's night we could see far more stars than I am able to see now from our Kansas City home. I suppose it was because there were no street or other bright lights. Also, the sky went to the horizon in any direction. In this vast half-globe we could see millions of stars and the Milky Way was a common part of the heavens.

The most fun on a hot night would be to watch the

sheet lightning or what we called "summer lightning" sweep across vast areas of the sky in the distance. This often meant that bad weather was brewing, but we knew that the storm wouldn't soon be upon us as long as the lightning was not flashing in sharp streaks followed by claps of thunder.

When thunder did begin to roll, we would count slowly from the time we saw the lightning flash until the thunder sounded as we had been told that the number we reached would indicate how many miles away the rain clouds were. Thus if we counted to 10, it would indicate the cloud wherein the lightning occurred was 10 miles in the distance. Obviously, when lightning and thunder were virtually simultaneous, the storm was upon us.

At the end of an extra hot summer evening, we would resort to makeshift arrangements in an attempt to have comfortable sleeping. We boys had a sanitary couch on the front porch. Our mother and dad would make a pallet of quilts spread on the front room floor between two open doors where there would be a draft. One thing we nearly always could depend on in Kansas was a breeze at night. My mother would sprinkle cold water on the sheet that was spread over the quilts. This helped to make the bed cool.

We had lots of quilts and "comforts." Everybody had them. They served a multitude of purposes, most notable of which was to provide extra beds on the floor when company arrived or for us on a hot summer night.

Before crawling into bed, we boys were reminded each and every night that we had to pump a basin of water and wash our feet. We had, of course, been barefoot all day. It was a cardinal rule that we couldn't go to bed with dirty feet no matter how tired we were.

Looking back, it becomes obvious that except for the lawn or porch swings, we didn't spend anything for summer furniture. We "made do" with what we had. But it must not have been very bad because we regarded summer as the most delightful part of the year. And the warm, summer evening was the best part of the day.

Watermelon,
Chicken and Summer

15

WATERMELONS are in the grocery stores in Kansas City almost all year around now, but my appetite seems to build up about late July, when the home grown crop from the Kaw Valley begins to hit the market.

Perhaps it's nostalgia, or maybe it's the memory of a time when tastebuds were more acute; but a home grown watermelon cooled in a tub of water at the pump on the porch was about the finest thing that nature ever created.

Most of our foods in pre-electricity days were seasonal; maybe that's why as each one came on the scene, it was a thrill. Fried chicken, for instance, was a summer treat only.

We had watermelon only when a farmer from the Kaw Valley hauled in a wagonload. When the first wagon hit Main Street sometime in July, it was big news. Small boys playing in the blacksmith shop ran home through hot dust that fairly seared their feet to announce to their mothers the watermelon man soon would be around.

And he would. Slowly, he'd drive up one street and down another—in Maple Hill this wasn't too much of a trip.

Our mothers would step out to the roadside to look at the melons as the farmer would pull back a canvas cover shielding them from the sun. The shiny green melons lay in a bed of straw in the wagon.

Each melon had its price.

"That one there," the farmer would say as he thumped it with his finger, "is worth a quarter. That big one over there in the corner is 35 cents. Plug 'em if you want me to. All guaranteed ripe."

At our house, we'd usually buy two. One would go to the cellar. The other immediately would be put in a tub of water freshly pumped from the well. By the time dad was home from the blacksmith shop it would be cool—not iced, of course.

The few times we got ice cold watermelon was when someone put one deep in the sawdust in an old ice house and left it for a day or two. Or you could buy ice-cold watermelon, 10 cents a slice, at the annual Kansas Free Fair at Topeka. The old ice house, incidentally, was about the first thing to succumb to the modern era of the motor car and truck.

A watermelon that is cold is better than one that is warm; that I'll concede. But I can't recall that any of us boys ever turned one down even if we picked it right out in the sun. Maybe it added to the fun, if you were eating the melon at a place where you could spit the seeds with abandon, or "squirt" them out with your fingers.

We usually washed at the pump after we had eaten watermelons.

The watermelon season ended almost abruptly soon after school started in September. By that time we'd had about all we could take. Also, they had lost some of their flavor. The watermelon growers over in the river valley would let the word get around that you could fill the back seat of your car with them for $2; choose them yourself. We boys would have one big picnic as sort of a celebration on the opening of school and to cash in on these cheap prices. But the watermelon had had its day and we were ready for something else.

Frying chickens, fortunately, came along about harvest time.

One summer an old Rhode Island Red hen hid her nest out back of our coal house and raised a brood of chickens. My brothers and I watched them grow as we fed them table scraps. Maybe it wasn't a balanced ration, but it sufficed.

We regarded a young rooster of about four pounds, somewhat larger than the birds commonly sold in the stores today, as a suitable fryer. The season wasn't prolonged, perhaps only through July and August. After that the chickens became too large for frying, and there was no more fried chicken until the next year.

Good as it was, fried chicken day after day could be monotonous.

It is difficult today to realize what a problem it was

to have fresh meat on the farm in the hot summer weather. In town we bought what we needed for each meal at the store.

Our wants, apparently, were simple. We bought a quarter's worth of steak, a nice little roast, or some boiling beef. That's all I recollect mother sending us to the store to get.

Obviously the butcher knew exactly what to cut for our family. He'd wrap it up in brown paper, we'd run home with it and Mom would put it in the skillet.

I have wondered since whatever happened to all the other cuts on the beef carcass. Surely the beef critter was made just as now, but I never heard of a sirloin steak, loin point roast, or all the other fancy names common in today's big chain stores. My recollections are the butcher heaved a big leg of beef from the cooler onto the heavy chopping block and started cutting on one end. He followed the simple process of cutting each order until it was all gone. I suppose that can't be right. I do know every order was cut as requested; there was no prepackaged meat.

Whenever we went to Topeka and got the thrill of eating in a restaurant, Dad looked the menu over but inevitably ordered roast beef. It cost 30 cents. He said you could always depend on roast beef so we never tried anything else.

Watermelons and fried chicken weren't the only things that came in season. There'd be cherries in early summer and we picked them from our trees or bought them a half bushel at a time, to be canned of course, But there'd always be a few fresh cherry pies. Lots of sugar because the fresh cherries would be tart. There just can't be anything in the world better.

Then the new potatoes seemed to come along at the same time as fresh peas. They were cooked together in a creamy sauce and you put real yellow butter on top and it kind of floated around.

There were weeks when we had fresh asparagus which was pulled from the patch that thrived from year to year in an out-of-the-way place in the garden. Rhubarb was in the same category, an early summer delicacy.

We even had some spartan-like fun when the horse-radish roots were dug and ground in the meat grinder on the back porch. Everybody "cried" tears during this process. We'd take turns at the handle of the grinder, vying to see who could take the strong fumes the longest. It was a game, too, the next day, to try the fresh horseradish on meat. We always thought a bite of the stuff would cure a summer cold.

String beans came on early and lasted late. We got tired of them.

Roasting ears came along in here somewhere. It wasn't always the sweet corn variety; but field corn picked at just the right moment was about as good. And the ears were bigger. We'd be watching the corn day by day, waiting for the first ears to be large enough for eating. We'd pull back the shucks and press the kernels to squeeze out the milk. When that day arrived, and for the next several days until the corn got too mature, we'd rival hogs in being corn fed.

I liked to roll the corn in butter on my plate, eat all the kernels, then roll the cob in the butter again and lick it off. It was one of the joys of the summer.

104

Summer's Best Treat

16

ALL this talk about the advantages of built-in "maid service" in the foods purchased at stores today—the ready-to-bake rolls, the TV dinners, the frozen french fried potatoes and a host of other items—actually would have been resented in my old home town.

The women in our town bragged about things that were homemade, and we youngsters were convinced that certain "store bought" foods lacked the luster and taste of those that our mothers produced.

Homemade ice cream is one example. It comes to mind now because this is the picnic season and homemade ice cream was a special treat. In fact, homemade ice cream and lemonade made a picnic as far as we youngsters were concerned. There was no trouble about the games to be played, or worry about supplies of other kinds of food, such as fried and pressed chicken, potato salad, and chocolate cake covered by thick layers of fudge frosting.

Homemade ice cream was an occasion. I can't say it was a rarity, because at Maple Hill most anything could be used to justify an occasion to be celebrated with a big dinner, picnic or otherwise. That situation still holds true today. When the *Alma Signal-Enterprise* reports in the Maple Hill news notes that delicious refreshments were served, that's exactly what is meant, then and now.

Summer time, particularly the hot days of August, was the time for homemade ice cream. You had to plan for it. For instance, when Maple Hill had an ice house, it was necessary for a brother and me to take our little wagon down to the place when it was open of a morning, to get a 50-pound chunk. The attendant shoveled off layers of sawdust from the big cakes of ice that had been cut from Mill Creek and stored during the winter.

Our family was one of many in town that didn't have an ice box. We felt very fortunate because we had a good well right at our back porch with a trap door at the top. It was easy to hang the milk and butter in a pail that was lowered on a rope almost to the surface of the cool water at the well's bottom. So we didn't go to the expense of buying ice, even some years later when it was delivered by truck from St. Marys.

When we hauled the ice home, it was put in a wash tub in the cellar and covered first with old newspapers and then gunny sacks, to keep out air and heat. Usually, the ice cream would be made later in the afternoon to be served at supper, or as an after-supper treat.

One reason, perhaps, that homemade ice cream was appreciated was that it took work. When the time arrived for this work to begin, we'd put the hunk of ice into an old gunny sack and crush it by beating on the sack with the flat side of an ax.

The freezer was set on the wooden wash bench, the one our mother set her wash tubs on. This bench was under a grape arbor just off the back porch. Our mother, of course, prepared the mix for the ice cream, and poured it into the container. We boys would pack ice and salt into the wooden freezer tub and then the work would begin in earnest.

We would turn the crank with great gusto at first. Then we'd turn, and turn, and turn, it seemed forever. Finally, when we were sure it was frozen solid and couldn't be budged further, our mother, a slender woman, would take hold of the crank and to our amazement would turn it for several minutes more.

Next we poured out the extra water in the freezer and packed in new ice; then let the ice cream "set" until the time it was to be served.

Incidentally, at our house such jobs as freezing ice cream were done without the assistance of our father. It was our mother's contention that a man who worked 10 hours a day six days a week in the blacksmith shop was not obligated to help with the cooking or the housework.

One of the nicest things about homemade ice cream back in the days before mechanical refrigeration was that you had to eat it all, once you started serving, because there was no way to keep it. We ate it all, one big bowl after another.

People said that was what was so good about homemade ice cream. You could eat until you were ready to pop, yet even the last bite tasted good. While this factory stuff, well, if you ate too much you began to get a slick taste on your tongue.

Still, it was a big thrill, in fact sort of a tradition, on a hot summer Saturday night to go downtown—everybody went downtown anyway—to have a dish of ice cream either at the drug store or in Jim Fyfe's restaurant, tobacco shop and pool hall. If the women folks were along, you usually went to the drug store to sit in the iron chairs at the little round tables.

This was the night the farm and town youngsters got together to play. We played on the street and on the sidewalks in front of the stores, while our parents were idling around visiting. All the while we knew that at some point in the evening we would suggest to our father and mother that maybe this was the time to have a dish of ice cream before going home. And they'd say, "Well, if we do, you boys will have to go home just as soon as we finish so you can get some sleep and be ready for Sunday School in the morning."

On a Sunday evening, especially if we had company, we'd get a quart of cream (60 cents, handpacked) at the drug store. My brother Bernard, who liked to show how fast he could run, would agree to get it. Our mother would have spoons and the bowls ready for immediate serving. You couldn't put what was left in the refrigerator because we had no refrigerator.

Canning for the Winter

THE sight in recent days of elderberries hanging heavily on bushes along rural roads in Missouri and Kansas was a reminder of the summer-long canning season we used to have.

My mother spent a good part of the summer and early fall filling the cellar for winter, and she did a good job.

The fact is, elderberries were of little significance, but they were plentiful and cheap. There were so many of them that it seemed a shame to let them go to waste even though they were a lot of bother. My brothers and I would walk a country road to a lane along the railroad tracks near Mill Creek east of town.

There we'd fill a tub with clusters of dark-purple berries. We could have easily picked 10 tubs, but one was all we could carry—and more than our mother really wanted to handle.

Removing the berries from the stems was a big job, and they stained everything they touched. But they made wonderful pies. The fresh berries were so juicy that it was almost impossible to make a pie in which the crust, both upper and lower, was not soaked.

No matter. The taste of the first couple of elderberry pies each season was wonderful, but we didn't want a steady diet of elderberry pies.

After making perhaps a couple of the pies, our mother would can the rest of the berries, filling two or three half-gallon jars for the winter.

We'd heard that there were other uses for elderberries—such as wine—but not at our house. There were two good reasons for this, one minor, the other major. The minor one was that it was against the law in Kansas to make wine and that would have been reason enough. The other was my mother's edict against anything alcoholic being in the house.

Elderberries, being a late-summer or early-fall crop, obviously didn't start the canning season. We began with cherries. Here, again, the first cherries from our trees went into a cherry pie. In our opinion—an opinion I still hold—no pie was quite equal to one made from cherries freshly picked from the tree, juicy enough to soak into the crust and run over the edge of the pie tin into the oven and tart enough to require a little sugar sprinkled on top.

That's even better than fresh peas and new potatoes, although potatoes are not a dessert and perhaps the two dishes shouldn't be compared.

Once the first pies had been enjoyed, the canning of the cherries began. With no sisters in the family, we boys had to help, although I wouldn't want to suggest that we performed important tasks. We could pit cherries and keep the coal bucket full so that the fire in the kitchen range was going all the time.

Canning over a coal range, incidentally, was hot work, but it was necessary work if you expected to have a cellar full of fruit in the winter. Women like my mother did such work as a matter of routine.

Canning meant kettles full of cooking fruit and dishpans of boiling water for sterilizing the jars. In all the canning tasks, we did as much as we could either out on the back porch or in the shade of a big tree just outside the kitchen door. But the cooking and the actual canning had to be done at the stove in the kitchen—no air conditioning, no electric fans.

We'd can perhaps a bushel or a bushel and a half of cherries. One year we borrowed a pitting machine, a little hand device. You fed the cherries into a hopper, turned a handle and the seed was rubbed from the cherry, the fruit dropping from one spout and the seed from another. It worked all right, but you still had to check the cherries to make sure a seed had not gone through with the fruit.

Next in line in the canning season came the gooseberries. The two bushes in our own garden supplied just enough berries for a couple of pies. But there was the Shorty Adams family that lived in a little old house on the Kaw River about three miles from Maple Hill. They needed money and they were hard workers. The children would pick wild gooseberries and bring them to town, selling them, if I recall correctly, at the ridiculously low price of $1 a bushel.

Of course, a dollar was a dollar in those days, but anyone who has ever picked a bushel of wild gooseberries knows they earned every penny they got.

My mother would buy half a bushel. Every little berry had to be stemmed, which suggests the reason for the limit of half a bushel, regardless of the price. The whole job was worth it only when you enjoyed the gooseberry pie in midwinter.

Through the summer came peaches, pickled peaches, peach preserves and peach butter. Then there were the blue plums. These plums didn't grow at Maple Hill, so the local grocer would inform all the housewives when he planned to receive a shipment. My mother, along with the other women of the town, bought plums at this time and canned them.

Along with peaches, plums were our favorite canned fruit. We had a big fruit bowl which looked like cut glass but wasn't. This bowl easily would hold the fruit from a two-quart jar. Throughout the winter, the bowl sat on the dining table most of the time. We had no refrigeration of any kind, but in the winter anything containing liquid would freeze if left in the dining room.

This was one reason we liked plums and peaches so much. In the morning you could take a big spoon and scrape the frozen plum or peach juice from the big bowl and it was just like ice cream.

This suggests, too, that we didn't regard the freezing as a hardship, but as an advantage. Once the fires in the kitchen range and in the big Round Oak stove in the front room got going full blast on a cold morning, the house would be warm enough.

Anything my mother didn't want frozen, such as milk, would be set by the fire in the front room on a cold winter night.

Somewhere along in the summer came the rhubarb preserves. My father, having come from Scotland, had a taste for orange marmalade. Somebody always gave us some for Christmas. My mother didn't care for it. Also, it was expensive.

She mixed up some kind of a rhubarb marmalade that not only was inexpensive, but was easily made. Since we consumed huge quantities of any kind of spread she offered us with her freshly baked bread, the rhubarb jam filled the bill.

The good bread and the tasty jams and jellies indicated how delicious things could complement each other. It was a pleasant family joke at our house that my father never could make the two come out equal. He always ended up with a little bread left so he'd have to have more jam. Then he'd take too much jam and that would require a little more bread.

Eating at our house was fun. I don't know whether my mother actually planned a balanced diet or whether it just came out that way. She knew, when the first cold winds blew, that we had plenty of fruit in the cellar for the winter—in a day when it wasn't always available at the store.

The strawberry preserves came soon after the cherries in early summer. Occasionally, we had apricots to can, but mostly they were frozen out in the spring.

In mid-September came the apples. Some farmer with an orchard would drive into town with a wagon of apples. He'd stop at the blacksmith shop where my father would buy one or two barrels to be dropped off at our house. They'd all be put in the cellar. We'd wrap the very best in pieces of newspaper and put them in baskets. Most of the others we'd spread out in a bin in the cellar.

The culls would be canned, or made into apple butter or jelly.

Nothing was prettier than apple jelly unless it was crab apple jelly. The latter was lighter in color, and when a glass of it was set in a window, the light shone through to make it the most appealing spread there was.

Jelly-making, like canning, was a hot job. It required peeling the fruit, the cooking in kettles on the hot stove and the boiling water for sterilizing the glasses. In addition, there was the melted paraffin which was poured over the top of the jelly glass to seal in the product. The paraffin also served as a tolerable chewing gum.

When the fruit juice had cooked on the stove, my mother would take a spoon of it and hold it high for a moment to let it cool. Then she would turn the spoon to let the juice drip back into the kettle. If the drips were in slow, thick drops, then the juice was ready to "jell."

The next step was to take a big spoon or dipper and skim off the layer of sediment that had formed on top the cooking juice. The "skim" would be put in a little bowl where it was available, as soon as it cooled, for us boys to eat with a spoon. Just an extra dividend on canning days.

When the juice in the kettle had cooled a little

more—if I recall correctly—it was strained through cloth or what was called a jelly bag. If you squeezed the bag to get the last drop of juice, likely you'd make the jelly cloudy.

Wild plums and wild grapes were among the fruits used for jelly. There were lots of plum thickets on roadsides around Maple Hill, but more often than not, insects got the biggest share. You had to be selective and we boys watched for the thickets where the quality of the fruit was the best.

Likewise, we'd locate the sources of wild grapes long before they were ripe. In a good year, getting a plentiful supply was no problem.

The winter larder would not have been complete without pickles and relishes. My mother was great on variety. She'd put up, for example, just a few jars of watermelon pickles.

Then there was chow-chow, a mixture of green tomatoes, cucumbers, red peppers, onions, string beans, cloves, pepper, salt and lots of vinegar. In recalling these canning seasons I wonder just how much vinegar we used at our house. We'd buy it by the jug at the grocery store. We bought sugar in 100-pound sacks.

Mustard pickles were among our favorites. They were made with green tomatoes, cucumbers, peppers and spices and covered with a mustard dressing.

Of course, there were the sweet cucumber pickles and the dills. For the dills, rather large cucumbers were sliced and layers of the sliced cucumbers put in a two-gallon jar with alternate layers of dill and grape leaves. Salt brine would be poured on, then my mother would put a plate on top and weight it down with a rock.

Piccalilli was another relish which included the inevitable green tomatoes, green peppers and onions.

The fact is tomatoes played a major role in canning.

Along late in August or the first week of September, everybody had tomatoes. I might not be remembering correctly, but I don't recall summers of tomato failures. Makes me wonder if all the new hybrids are really an improvement over what we once grew in the farm gardens.

What I do recall is that late in the summer, tomatoes were sold by the bushel, not the pound. If you weren't careful, friends would load you up with more tomatoes then you could use.

It was while they were this plentiful that my mother capped the season by making chili sauce—with tomatoes, onions, red peppers, celery seed, cloves, cinnamon, allspice, nutmeg. While it was cooking on the stove, it gave forth the most delightful aroma imaginable.

Some people, if asked, might say that the most pleasing fragrance that you could get would be from Chanel No. 5.

Not me, I'll take the aroma from chili sauce cooking on a stove any time.

New Sidewalks

18

THE current city craze for skateboards is a reminder that we used to have similar fads in our old home town.

One of ours, as I recall, was roller skates, although up to this particular time in our childhood, they had been out of the question in a small town with no paved sidewalks. But circumstances developed that made it possible for us to enjoy this form of recreation.

I have a faint recollection of board sidewalks in Maple Hill, at least in the downtown area—one block. Recollections are much more vivid of a concrete sidewalk building spree in the town when not only were board walks replaced, but sidewalks were laid where there never had been any before.

There must have been an era of rural prosperity or perhaps a surge of civic spirit. At any rate sidewalks were built all over town. It seems the town had passed an ordinance which provided that each block was to have a sidewalk on one side of the street or the other so that anybody could walk on concrete to the postoffice.

So we had new sidewalks from the Rock Island railroad depot at the far south edge of town to the home of the banker, Frank Adams, at the far north end. Some of the sidewalks not only went beside vacant lots, but just plain pasture.

The sidewalks were smooth and obviously inviting for skating. I don't recall who started it, but in no time at all most of the town kids had skates.

In that era the town kids were set apart from the farm kids in many respects, one of them being this opportunity to roller skate. You couldn't do that in the mud of a farm yard, or even on the stone walk from the back porch to the barn. Boys and girls on the farm often envied us in town, even in such a town as Maple Hill with only 250 people.

In this roller skating spree, we learned there were two kinds of skates—Those with ball bearings in the iron wheels, and those without. Some of the older girls got the ballbearing kind, but most of the boys my age got the cheaper ones.

To any onlooker, it was obvious the girls were much better skaters than the boys. In fact, they'd chide us on our system of skating which was to shove one foot straight forward and then the other. There was no rhythm of motion for coasting. We either forcefully propelled the iron wheels on the iron axles or we didn't move.

Eventually our parents realized the handicap under which we boys were operating and we got ballbearing

119

skates. What a revelation in ease of motion.

The skate fad passed when we took the skate wheels for the making of scooters. These resembled the current skateboards except they had a front-post onto which you could hold with both hands as you propelled yourself down the sidewalk with one foot.

Our sidewalks were ideal also for coaster wagons and we could coast for blocks. My father was a blacksmith and he liked things that were sturdy. Most everything he made was braced with iron. He built a wren house once and my mother smilingly commented that it would hold an eagle.

So when my father bought a coaster wagon he got a good stout one. He sent to the Stowe Supply Company in Kansas City which was where he always bought such things, along with blacksmith shop supplies.

The wagon had a wooden body and iron wheels. Best of all, the wheels had roller bearings. My brother, Bernard, and I, near the same age, immediately developed a system of riding in the wagon, one which I don't see used any more. The driver rested his weight on his right knee in the front left side of the wagon and held the tongue of the wagon in his right hand. The other rider put his left knee in the wagon at the right rear and used his right foot to help propel it.

We worked our pushing legs in unison and could make the wagon fly on a downhill run. Our younger brother, Don, who was about 3 at the time, sometimes would sit in the middle of the wagon. He had long, blond curls which flew in the wind as he hung on for dear life. Neighbors used to wonder why Fanny Turnbull would let her boys take that baby in that wagon that way. But as far as I can recall, he never got hurt—at least not badly.

One reason our wagons were such good coasters was that we kept them well oiled. We learned around the blacksmith shop that moving parts on any machine should be lubricated. And we had plenty of oil; in fact, an oversupply.

The big gasoline engine in the blacksmith shop that powered the blower at the forge, the emery wheels, the drill and disk sharpener had a bearing that floated in oil. This oil had a tendency to drip on the shop floor so my father placed a gallon can at the point of the drip to catch it. The can was nearly always full of oil.

We'd fill a Prince Albert tobacco can with the oil and proceed to pour it on the wheels of our wagons. We did the same to our roller skates. In addition to the fact the oil was at the shop, we were instructed to do our lubricating there because oil dripped from the wheels of both skates and wagons and people didn't like their sidewalks spotted in front of their homes.

If housewives today could have heard our iron-wheeled wagon going pell-mell down the sidewalk, they'd probably better appreciate today's rubber-tired toys. Since we and other boys with their wagons roamed all over town, the noise wasn't confined to any one area. Incidentally, when we were small, although there were a few cars in town, our parents didn't live under the constant fear that we might get out into the street and be run over. Not only were the cars few, but the roads were dirt and there was little speeding.

One test for the sturdiness of our coaster wagon was made where the sidewalk came to an end down the street from our house. There was a dropoff of about a foot to the earth pathway that led to the road.

Bernard and I would start up the slope half a block away to build up steam as we propelled the wagon toward that dropoff. We hit it as fast as we could go and the wagon would thump the ground as we left the sidewalk.

When I was a youngster there were, as I recall, two bicycles in town. Allan Weaver's father bought him a new one and John Carlson somehow got hold of a used bike. With only two bicycles, they couldn't be a fad. That was to come later. By the time Don was 10 or 11 years old, nearly all the boys in Maple Hill had bikes and they rode to Rossville and Willard to see boys in those towns who had bikes, something we never would have thought of doing just a few years before.

The young men in the town, however—at least some of the more adventurous—had motorcycles. Riding a motorcycle on a country road was an adventure, particularly if you got in a rut.

The main street in Maple Hill in the downtown block usually was the smoothest street in town. It was, therefore, a chosen place for getting motorcycles started. The method of starting was to put the cycle in gear, run along beside it while pushing it and then, when the motor started, to jump on the saddle and roar away.

Such events usually could draw a crowd of small and admiring boys, who longed for the day when they could have a motorcycle.

Bernard and I eventually came into possession of a motorbike that had seen better days. The motor wouldn't run and the tires were flat. But we could propel it with the pedals just like a bicycle.

At this point, we graduated from the coaster wagon and willed it to Don. We took the useless motor and tires off the motorbike. It was rather difficult sitting in the wide saddle seat and pumping the pedals that would make it run on the wheel rims, but we did pretty well going downhill on the sidewalk. I'm sure even the most tolerant of our neighbors would have welcomed a return to the iron-wheeled wagon.

Somehow, we always had fun with any kind of wheels. And older men loitering around the blacksmith shop would tell us how they, as boys, used old buggy wheels to make carts and other devices.

One story was about a group who put a little platform on an old buggy chassis and tied ropes to the front axles to be used to guide the vehicle. They took the old chassis to the top of the big hill west of town, loaded as many boys as they could on the little platform, and let her start rolling down the slope.

As one of the story tellers—my Uncle Walt—recalled, they learned in a hurry they had miscalculated on what speed would develop. Faster and faster they went down the hill. Ahead was a barbed wire fence, but the old buggy chassis had no brakes. The speed was so great the boys were afraid to jump off, so they hit the fence head on. The fence wires broke, a buggy wheel collapsed and several of the boys were badly scratched.

This turned out to be a one-time adventure. After hearing about it, it was one experiment with wheels that the boys in my group never tried.

Boys and Boats

19

THOSE early explorers who reported after crossing Kansas that it was part of the Great American Desert no doubt would be flabbergasted today if on a weekend they saw the long lines of cars pulling motorboats down the highways.

Doubtless the early settlers who fought droughts and grasshoppers hardly would believe their eyes if they could return and view such vast bodies of water as the Tuttle Creek Reservoir and see on them powerful, speedy boats towing skiers over windblown waves.

To be sure, it's all part of a new era, but shucks, we had boats on Mill Creek in Kansas when I was a boy. Nobody referred to our liking for boats as a "boat craze" nor was a boat a status symbol, but we had a lot of fun with them just the same.

Admittedly, the boats we boys had were not sleek, plastic streamlined creations with mahogany woodwork and red seat covers. But they did have one thing in common with today's exotic speedsters—they floated, or at least most of the time.

There were several boats on Mill Creek, all owned by fishermen, some who lived in our town of Maple Hill, some in Topeka and some were farmers on farms through which the creek flowed.

Mill Creek circled our town about a mile distant on its way to the Kaw River. It wasn't the custom for boys to own a boat, perhaps because few had the money to buy one.

My first experience with a boat was with my cousin, Tom Romick. The Rock Island railroad right-of-way divided the Romick farm. On either side of the tracks there was a slough and when we had a series of wet years the slough would be full of water, creating a lake of several acres.

It was in one of those wet years that one of Tom's relatives who had a farm on the creek found an abandoned boat. It was a little green boat and though we were small lads, we managed to get it into the slough.

The boat's equipment consisted of two or three flat boards to be used as paddles and two or three tin cans to bail out the water. The cans were as necessary as the paddles.

The slough was not more than two or three feet deep, so there was no danger. We paddled our way up and down, watched the trains go by and had a good time in general.

The weather in June that year was cold and wet. Since none of us boys ever had any such thing as a rain coat, we just put on any old coat or sweater for some protection against the elements. And we always were barefoot. So we'd ride in the boat when it was pouring down rain, huddled in a coat, our bare feet in water up to the ankles, one boy paddling or poling the craft while the other bailed.

We even tried making a sail, but our Kansas seafaring experience was not sufficient to give us the proper skills. The sail never worked.

Surmising that where there was water there might be fish, Tom, by brother, Bernard, and I decided we'd see if we could catch some. A barbed wire fence ran through the slough parallel to the railroad tracks. Using the boat to get to the fence, we tied short lines with hooks on them to the fence wires. Then we baited the hooks with long, wiggly worms which could be found by the jillions in the muddy soil along the edge of the slough.

We were surprised—and jubilant—to catch several husky bullheads. From then on through the summer the slough provided excellent fishing for every one in town who liked to fish—for bullheads, carp and sunfish. The fish, presumably, had entered the slough at some time when Mill Creek was flooding and creek water had cut across the country, following the railroad right-of-way.

My experience with Tom and his boat made me want one of my own. The opportunity came when Mill Creek flooded again and Edwin Thompson, a farm boy whose farm was on the creek, caught a boat which had pulled away from its moorings some place upstream. Edwin had a good boat of his own and also a canoe. He had real oars for his boat and "boughten" paddles for his canoe. Obviously, this made him one of the elite on Mill Creek.

The boat Edwin had caught in the flood didn't quite equal his specifications, nor could he find the rightful owner. So he offered it to me for $1 and I bought it immediately.

This was a good deal all around. I certainly was glad to get the boat for $1 and Edwin, considering what the boat was like, was happy to sell at that price.

Edwin let me put my boat on the creek at a "dock" on his farm. This was a place where the weeds had been cut from the creek bank, giving good access to the water.

This boat had one thing in common with Tom's. It leaked water. Frankly, this wasn't a particular hardship because we had so much fun making repairs. The repairs cost nothing. I could get roofing tar at the blacksmith shop free.

There was a reason. My father was the blacksmith, and he was reasonably tolerant of boys around the shop. But he had to work, and work hard. When we boys got too rambunctious around home, our mother would tell us to go play at the blacksmith shop.

At the shop, Dad would say, "now see here, you boys. I don't care what you do, but keep out from under my feet."

An admonition of this kind was easy to comply with. It was why we were able to smoke out behind the shop while at home we would have been detected in a minute.

A horse shoer's rasp (file) has one side which is

deeply grooved. This is to enable him to trim the hoof rapidly. With such a rasp you could file a pine board and come up with flaky sawdust about the size of the makings for pipe tobacco.

For a penny you could buy a clay pipe with bamboo stem at Dave Stewart's store.

We'd use the sawdust in these pipes, but puff as hard as we could it just wouldn't work satisfactorily. So we switched to cigar butts. When my father was working at the anvil or shoeing a horse, he didn't have time to light a cigar. But he liked to hold one between his teeth. He'd bite away at it until it would get too short for comfort, then lay it on the edge of the forge to be forgotten.

I often have wondered if the reason I don't smoke today stems from the early experience of smoking those old cigar butts in clay pipes behind the blacksmith shop.

As previously indicated, this loose supervision which we were under at the blacksmith shop contributed to the free tar for the boat. The blacksmith shop roof had to be tarred occasionally and my father kept a barrel of the stuff in the coal shed. Without interfering with his work in any way, we'd turn the spout, fill a gallon paint can and head for the boat.

It was about two miles to the creek where we had the boat tied, most of the route being along the railroad track. We'd walk the rails barefoot, taking turns carrying the gallon of tar.

At the creek we'd pull the boat from the water, smear on the tar with a stick and rag. Sometimes we'd make two trips a day. The boat eventually got kind of heavy on the bottom side because of the tar.

We fashioned our paddles at the blacksmith shop and we learned how to paddle "Indian fashion," twisting the paddle at the end of each stroke so that the boat would go straight down the creek and not in circles.

A good part of the time, however, the boat was upside down. We'd paddle around for a while, then take off our clothes, put them on the bank and turn the boat over. We got a real thrill out of the phenomenon of the air space that would be created under the boat as it floated wrong side up. With the bottom of the boat as a diving platform, we'd jump into the water and swim under the boat. There, with our heads sticking up into the air space we could shout to each other. Really, this was lots more fun than paddling up and down the creek.

The water in the creek was deep—anywhere from 4 feet up to 14. Naturally, we picked the deep spots for our diving and tricks with the boat. I can't recall ever wondering if someone would see us as we played on the boat—not only without the tops of our bathing suits, but also the bottoms. In fact, nobody owned a bathing suit.

With the boat, we also set trot lines across the creek and it was on such a line across one of the deepest holes that I caught a 28-pound catfish.

My mother liked to fish but she had a mortal fear of water. Her fishing was entirely the kind where you sat on the bank with a long bamboo pole.

As I grew older I wondered how she permitted my brothers and I to spend so much time on the creek when she, herself, was dead certain that if you got out into the water you were going to drown. Of course, she wasn't aware how we played with the overturned boat, naturally assuming we rowed the thing up and down the creek.

Bernard and I wanted in the worst way to get our mother to take just one ride in the boat. She went with us one day to the creek to get walnuts and of course the best trees were on the other side. We argued and pleaded and she finally agreed that she would get in if we would paddle straight across to the other bank.

Admittedly, the boat did ride a little low in the water. But we had bailed it out before we let her in. She sat in the middle seat and held on tightly to each side as we paddled straight across, Bernard in the front and I at the back.

It was quite a triumph for us. But we never tried it again. Supposing it had sunk? She couldn't swim a stroke.

Of course, with us it was different. For instance, many a summer evening we went to the creek to seine minnows for J. D. Weaver, Brick Weaver's dad. Mr. Weaver set a trot line nearly every night. He liked for us boys to catch the minnows, but he didn't let us ride in his boat. After we had seined the minnows, we'd swim, while he baited his hooks.

When people asked him if he was worried about us boys, his reply would be:

"No. They're a bunch of damn ducks."

Owning a boat created some responsibilities. I soon found that people would borrow it without asking. In an effort to stop this, I got an old padlock from the blacksmith shop and locked the boat chain around the root of a tree. Much to my surprise, people would chop the root in two.

My trouble mainly was in the fall with hunters who wanted to get on the other side of the creek. While in school I couldn't watch the boat as closely as necessary and often on a Saturday I'd have to walk miles along the creek to locate it.

After one interval, I couldn't find it at all. My $1 investment had vanished, padlock and all.

But I still can say I once owned a boat. No captain was ever more proud.

Before the Combine

20

I<small>T IS</small> a good thing Kansas is no longer in the horse and buggy days. If farmers still used the harvest methods practiced when I was a boy, they just couldn't get the job done. Crops are too big. In fact, moving the millions of bushels of grain garnered has become a bigger problem than the harvest itself.

Many small elevators already have been eliminated and numerous railroad branch lines abandoned as farming and transportation have been modernized over the years. But any talk about additional reductions along this line becomes extremely controversial. Farmers and the little towns don't relish any further depreciation of services and they are prepared to fight such efforts.

Yet it is true that hauling wheat to town in a wagon was a slow process. The great and traditional harvest rush, as it was known in the days of the binder,

134

threshing machine and wagon, was a lot of exciting work but compared to today's methods it was pretty slow.

Because it brought whole communities together with a concentration on one job—that of getting the wheat to market—the harvest was the most exciting time of the year on the farm.

The harvest started at Maple Hill with the horse-drawn binders cutting and tying the wheat into bundles with work crews putting the bundles into shocks. The header, a big machine which just clipped the heads from the standing wheat and put those into a wagon to be hauled to the threshing machine or stacker, was not used in our part of Kansas. It was, however, the dominant machine in the big wheat country of western Kansas.

We boys who along with men were hired to shock wheat always worried that we would have to work on the Fourth of July. No celebration was important enough to stop the harvest. We always, of course, could go to any events which were held at night on the Fourth. And we always could hope that it would rain the night of the third, thereby delaying the harvest for one day.

Once the wheat was shocked, it awaited the threshing machine. Usually, in the Maple Hill area, two threshing outfits worked through the harvest season, starting soon after the grain was in the shock and continuing until about the first of September. The threshers went from farm to farm and their crews went with them.

The threshing crew consisted of the engineer for the

big steam engine, the separator (threshing machine) man, who often was the owner of the outfit, two men with pitchforks in the field to pitch the bundles of wheat onto hayracks to be hauled to the separator, six drivers for the hayracks who would pitch the bundles into the separator, a water boy, and drivers for wagons to haul the threshed wheat into town or to a bin. The owner of the farm usually was one of these drivers.

An outfit of this size working with a separator with a 36-inch cylinder (the workings of the inner part of the thresher that actually separated the wheat from the straw), could thresh about 1,000 bushels on a good day. As I recall, the 36-inch separators were about as big as we had at Maple Hill. There were smaller machines with 30-inch cylinders. In western Kansas some were as big as 42 inches.

A common thing to do was to haul the wheat directly from the threshing machine to town. The ordinary wagon box held about 40 bushels of wheat or even 60, but this was a big load for one team of horses to pull.

If we would assume that a farm was four miles from town, it took the farmer an hour to get from the threshing machine to Maple Hill. His first stop, at the time I was a boy, would have been at J. D. Weaver's scales. Weaver was a local buyer of wheat who ordered in the boxcars on the Rock Island railroad during the harvest season.

The loaded wagon weighed, the farmer would drive his team the short distance to the railroad tracks where he would proceed to scoop the wheat from his wagon into a boxcar. A husky farmer could get more than a peck, sometimes half a bushel, into one hefty scoop. But under the best of circumstances, getting his wagon in place and all, it would require nearly 30 minutes to unload a wagon. Then he had to go back to the scales to weigh the empty wagon before making the return trip home.

Thus it was that on an eight-mile round trip, the farmer would spend two and one-half to three hours delivering 40 bushels of wheat.

Many towns had elevators where a farmer could push the wheat from his wagon into a pit from which it was elevated into bins. Maple Hill had an elevator, too, but at that time it was owned by a rancher, W. J. Tod, who used it to store corn for his cattle-feeding operations. He wasn't in the business of merchandising wheat.

Where the wheat was loaded into an elevator, that facility loaded it into the boxcars thereby eliminating one scooping job.

With or without an elevator, the farmer had to make the trip from his farm to town at the four-mile-an-hour rate.

As I recall, not too many farmers at Maple Hill had bins in which they could store wheat at threshing time. However, if they did this it meant scooping the grain into the bin from the wagon and then scooping it out again when it came time to ship to market. It still had to go to the boxcar on the railroad tracks in town.

Farmers who did not want to market during the harvest rush would stack their wheat. Wheat that was to be stacked could be cut with the binder just a little earlier than that which was going to be threshed directly.

The stacked wheat went through a "sweat" which improved the quality. People used to talk about certain farmers who always had the best quality wheat because they stacked it.

But stacking, of course, involved another operation. First the wheat was shocked and then it was hauled on hayracks to an area where the stacks were to be erected. Nearly every community, Maple Hill included, had a couple of fellows, usually old-timers, who were experts at stacking.

For their day, they got a specialist's wage, up to $10.

The stacker knew how to place the bundles, one on top of the other so that he would end up with the center of the stack a little higher than the outer edges. And yet, the bundles were placed so that each acted to hold the other in place about like shingles on a roof. This meant that the stack would stand firm, would not spread apart and would shed rain.

Once the stack was made, it could stand for months. This gave the farmer the opportunity to choose his time of threshing, and, of course, permitted him to market after the harvest rush. Farmers used to think, perhaps with justification, that wheat prices always were lowest at harvest time when they were selling.

In stacking wheat, farmers would build the stacks in pairs with just enough room between them for the threshing machine.

The bundles of wheat were tossed with pitchforks directly from the stack into the separator.

The grain still had to be hauled to town in a wagon.

It was a great boon to the harvest when the first trucks began to appear on the scene. This transition began when I was a teen-ager.

Later, of course, the entire harvest system was changed by the advent of the combine.

A single big combine now can harvest thousands of bushels a day in a field where not too many turn arounds are required. Trucks hauling 200 to 300 bushels can make the trip to the elevator in a hurry.

If you make the comparison with the two and a half to four hours that it took the farmer at Maple Hill when I was a boy to get 40 bushels of wheat four miles into town, you can imagine what today's trucks could do in the same time.

Such comparisons really aren't valid under today's conditions, but they do help emphasize how vast the changes have been in harvesting methods. And it is a good thing the changes have come or current crops wouldn't be in the bin by Christmas.

Threshing Days

21

HEARING the annual complaints of the boxcar shortage in recent Kansas harvests, I am reminded that this was one trouble we didn't have when we were threshing wheat back in my old home.

Boxcars were used, of course, just as they are now, but the Rock Island railroad apparently always had enough on hand to set them on the side tracks at Maple Hill when they were needed. The point is, we didn't need as many all at once back in the days when the grain was threshed as they do now when it is combined in the fields.

Kansas now will combine as much as 200 million bushels of wheat in two weeks, but it would have taken all summer and fall to have threshed that much back when I was a small boy.

The harvest season at Maple Hill was a busy several weeks for nearly everybody in town as well as on the farm. My father was kept busy in his blacksmith shop, shoeing horses, making repairs on binders and resetting wagon tires.

The two little grocery stores had an upsurge in business as they supplied food products to the farms where harvest crews were at work. The icehouse was busy supplying ice to farms which treated workers to iced tea—one of the extras that went with the big harvest dinners.

For farm wives and daughters, of course, it was the busiest time of the year, feeding those hungry harvest crews.

All of the men of the town who did work by the day for a living were engaged in the harvest and always there were outsiders who came for jobs. High school boys earned their winter spending money in this season.

On Saturday night, everybody came to town. It would be after midnight before Jack Herron, the barber, could give every man a haircut and a shave. Meanwhile, the wives visited the stores. It was a busy, exciting and good time to be alive.

My first experience in the harvest started with boxcars—that's why boxcar shortages strike a personal chord with me. The railroad was our contact with the outer world at Maple Hill and everything about it—including the boxcars—was exciting to the boys of my age.

That's how it happened that we became involved in the harvest activities when we were only 9 or 10 years old.

Allan (Brick) Weaver, my brother Bernard and

myself, along with one or two other lads were hired to shovel the wheat to the ends of the boxcars after it had been scooped into them by farmers. We got the job because Brick's dad, J. D. Weaver, was the local buyer of the wheat.

Mr. Weaver (we accorded the title "mister" to all men) paid us 10 cents a day, in pennies. But money wasn't the lure; it was the fact you could spend a day in boxcars, even riding in them when the local freight pulled them from one location to another on the siding. Occasionally, you could even hang on the iron ladder on the side of the car and give the engineer the highball.

Why our mothers let us do this I'll never understand. The only explanation I can think of today is that they didn't know what we were doing and our fathers were too busy to pay any attention. Frankly, though, none of us was ever hurt. The fact was that everybody from the agent at the depot to the farmers knew us personally, so we probably were watched over far more than we imagined.

When a farmer was selling wheat directly from the threshing machine, the grain was loaded into a wagon from the separator. When the wagon was filled a team would be hitched to it and it would be pulled away as another empty wagon was put in its place.

The farmer, or one of his hired men, would drive the team and wagon into Maple Hill where the wagon would be weighed on Fairbanks scales at the feed store. Then the farmer would drive the wagon to the railroad siding where a boxcar would be waiting.

A wooden chute would be hooked over the side of

the wagon and over boards across the door of the boxcar. This chute had sides on it to keep wheat from falling to the ground as the farmer scooped his load into the car.

As I recall, a good wagon held 40 to 60 bushels of wheat. A scoop would pick up about 20 pounds or a third of a bushel. It took a man with strong arms and back to unload a wagon in this manner. As he scooped, the wheat fell into the center of the boxcar and it was the job of us boys to push it toward either end.

The cars would be filled to a depth of 4 or 5 feet. This would be about 1,800 bushels, so it took a lot of wagons to fill the one car.

After a farmer had emptied his wagon, he would return it to the scales to be weighed again. The difference between the loaded and unloaded weights would reveal the amount of wheat he had hauled. Mr. Weaver would make out a slip and credit his account.

By the time the farmer got back to the threshing machine, another wagon would be filled. The process of hitching the team to the loaded wagon and pushing an empty vehicle under the spout of the separator would be repeated.

The number of wagons that actually would be employed in hauling the wheat to town would depend on yield of the crop (how fast it was coming out of the separator) and the distance from the farm to Maple Hill.

Mr. Weaver could be buying wheat from more than one farmer at a time, so many wagons might be crossing the scales each day to fill the waiting boxcars.

But it is obvious, in retrospect, that we didn't put much pressure on the Rock Island. It seems to me now that we filled about one car a day and that in late afternoon the loaded car would be moved to a side track where it could be picked up by an engine the next morning.

Meanwhile, another empty would be pushed into place for loading. It was these moves that gave us our rides.

We small boys had another way to cash in on the harvest in addition to our dime-a-day wage. No matter how careful a man was in scooping wheat into the boxcar, a little of it always spilled onto the packed cinder roadway along the tracks.

We boys "scooped" up this grain with our hands and put it into gunny sacks. Then we'd take it some place where there was a concrete sidewalk and rethresh it by tossing handfuls of it into the air.

In this manner, we'd come up with a fairly clean product that was good chicken feed and could be sold at bargain prices to folks in town who had back-yard flocks of hens.

One steady customer was Grandma Beaubein, an elderly widow who ran a boarding house, kept chickens and tended a garden.

Grandma Beaubein, about 5 feet tall, was a frugal woman who always had money in a little leather pouch which she carried in a dress pocket beneath her apron.

In case dogs bothered her chickens, she also carried a revolver under her apron and she not only knew how to shoot, but she would.

Grandma Beaubein was one of the early settlers at Maple Hill. She had come to this country from France as a young woman with a young husband who was suffering from tuberculosis. They'd heard that the dry weather of Kansas might cure the disease.

It didn't work and Mrs. Beaubein was left on her own to rear their children. She later helped with the upbringing of some of her grandchildren—with the income from her boarding house, garden and chickens.

Some official at Topeka repeatedly insisted that Grandma Beaubein was running a hotel and had to have a license. He would ride out on the train, hang up a hotel sign over the front door and issue all kinds of official pronouncements.

As soon as he got onto the train to return to the capital city, Grandma Beaubein took the sign down. She always argued that she was just keeping house for some boarders who needed a place to stay and didn't cater to the transient trade. The town agreed with her stand.

The fact was, Grandma Beaubein had to be careful with her money, something else the people in Maple Hill understood. But she never failed to pay a bill she owed.

We knew this, too, when we bargained with her over a half sack of salvaged wheat. When the price was agreed upon, she would reach under that apron, untie the little leather pouch and give us the cash. It was a good business deal all around.

We could salvage wheat even when we weren't working in the boxcars. We also could get corn when farmers were loading cars later in the fall.

Human nature being then about as it is now, when two boys went together to pick up grain at the boxcars, they'd get along fine. Add one more and you had competitive trouble as two nearly always would side against one.

Sometimes farmers would load boxcars from both sides. It could happen that more grain would be spilled on one side than the other. A fight would start as to which boys got access to the bigger supply on the ground.

In one such instance, I was being bested by two larger boys. One farmer, sensing that the fight wasn't on an equal basis, gave me the eye and motioned for me to bring my sack to the edge of his wagon. He put a full scoop of bright yellow corn into my sack—no cinders, no dirt, just good clean corn—pure gold, perhaps 15 cents worth.

I was forever grateful and never had a moment's remorse for the city elevator somewhere that was short-changed 20 pounds of corn.

A few years after our experience shoveling the wheat back in the boxcars, the other boys in my group and I were "graduated" into following the binder and shocking wheat.

A little later we were big enough and old enough to run the bundle wagons that hauled the wheat from the shocks to the threshing machines. We had our teams and our hayracks and were recognized as full hands in the harvest.

My harvest days ended when I was graduated from high school and started working fulltime in the blacksmith shop. From the shop I gravitated to *The Kansas City Star* as a reporter.

But no matter, the old-time glamour of the harvest was fading fast. The truck took over from the team and wagon and the combine replaced the binder.

The combine cut and threshed the wheat in one operation, eliminating the need for the crews to shock and then thresh the wheat—and the necessity also for the big farm dinners.

The combines could accomplish in a day what took a week under the older methods.

But they also have helped to create the biggest problem of the harvest—the boxcar shortage.

Fun on the Farm

22

GET two men together in the city who were reared back on the farm and almost invariably they'll start bragging about how hard they had to work when they were boys. They did. But they also had a lot of fun, most of it of their own making.

When I was a lad back in Maple Hill, almost every boy got a job on a farm in the summer to make some extra money. There were jobs by the day in the hayfields, cultivating corn and shocking wheat. As the boys got older, a few got jobs "by the month."

My first such job came when I was either 15 or 16. My employers were Mr. and Mrs. Will Romick, but I actually was hired by their son, Lawrence Romick. I was well acquainted with the family, of course. My father and mother were good friends of the Romicks and called them Will and Lou, just as they called my folks, John and Fannie. Since it didn't sound well for me to speak of Mr. and Mrs. Romick so informally, I was taught to say Uncle Will and Aunt Lou.

The Romicks had lived on a farm just about half a mile from Maple Hill while Lawrence and his sister, Edna, were small children. Lawrence was a few years older than I, Edna just a year or so older. Although he lived close to the farm, Lawrence managed somehow on his own to lead a very interesting life. He once killed five ducks with an old single-barrel 12-gauge shotgun with one shot, having hidden in the tall grass at the edge of a pond and waited until the birds were lined up just exactly right before he fired.

I was about 10 and John Carlson about 12 when Lawrence would drive by in a buggy at 4:30 a. m. to take us to Mill Creek to run bank lines which we had set the night before. John, a neighbor, and I slept on our front porches, so when Lawrence came by we could slip away without bothering our families. We would be back in time for breakfast.

For bait we often used baby mice which we could catch in the feed bin of Romick's barn by moving sacks of grain and disturbing the mice nests.

The Romicks later moved to a farm about four miles from town. Lawrence and I had a deal whereby he trapped and shot rabbits, cleaned them and brought them to school with him in the morning. I sold them and we split the money. Lawrence was a good trapper, too, and caught so many skunks that we nicknamed him "Nunks."

Lawrence found it amusing, along with some other young trappers, to throw his trapping gloves in the back part of empty desks in the school. The teacher could walk up and down the aisles trying to find "that boy" and if she had found him, she would have sent him home to change clothes. We boys thought this was a great joke; the girls thought it was awful.

One winter day, several of us arrived at the Romick farm to join Lawrence for a rabbit hunt. Lawrence directed us all to stand looking to the south, while he went to the garden at the north of the house. While making us promise not to look around, he dug into a pit to get apples. He didn't want that gang of boys to know where the pit was.

The barn on the Romick farm was across the road and a hundred yards or more from the house. As we left to hunt, heading first for the barn, Aunt Lou cautioned us to be careful and had half a dozen "don'ts." Aunt Lou was strict and Uncle Will even more strict. Uncle Will didn't even let Lawrence go to town on Saturday nights—the one night when nearly all farm youngsters had that privilege.

But we were out of sight at the barn. Lawrence led us inside to a dark manger and there under a feed box introduced us to his private domain. In it were a little .22-caliber revolver, a hunting knife such as we all had seen in the mail order catalogues, and a cache of chewing tobacco. We took everything along.

We lined our shotguns against a fence as each dared the other to take a "chaw." Nobody took a dare, although later we all wished we had. However, none got as sick as the old stories go. Our stomachs just didn't feel good.

Later, in the high grass around an old pond, the dogs began to get the rabbits running and each of us pulled up our shotguns to shoot. Not a gun fired. While we were taking our chaws, Lawrence had secretly un-loaded each gun, and of course was having a big laugh.

The night Lawrence was graduated from high school in Maple Hill he walked directly from the ceremonies which had been held at the church, down to Jim Fyfe's restaurant and pool hall. There he bought a big cigar. He walked up and down Main Street puffing that cigar and while I was gazing with awe at this brave act of manliness, he asked me if I would like to work on his farm, "by the month" for the summer. I said I would. The pay was to be $40 a month.

By this time, the Romicks had moved to a big farm near Dover, Kansas. It was about 14 miles from Maple Hill and a like distance from Topeka. Since they did not trade in Dover, we were for all practical purposes 14 miles in the country and we didn't see town except on Sundays. On that day my folks always got me to spend the day at home.

I was one of the family on the farm—this was true of most Maple Hill boys who got jobs by the month with their friends. I worked hard, but so did Lawrence and his Dad. There was no favoritism. Our day started pretty early as we milked four or five cows, fed and harnessed the horses, ate breakfast and were ready to be in the fields at 7.

One of my first tasks was cultivating corn. Lawrence and I had two-row walking cultivators. A lot of the corn acreage was old apple orchard ground which still contained many old stumps. We broke a host of breaking pins on the cultivators and each evening would whittle out a pocketful from sticks of hedge. The hedge would withstand as much pressure as anything but a steel bolt; using a bolt obviously would have meant a bent cultivator shank and a trip to the blacksmith shop.

I walked behind the cultivator 13 consecutive days, from 7 a. m. until 6 p. m. (time off for dinner at noon, of course). Neither Lawrence nor I thought this was particularly tough. I have tried to tell the story to my son who, with his friends, doesn't like to walk around the block. But he refuses to be properly impressed.

From cultivating corn we went to putting up hay and this was harder yet as we handled it with a pitchfork. In fact, we were glad to get back to the corn. From haying and corn we went into the wheat harvest, which was still harder. Lawrence drove the four-horse team to the binder. A young fellow who had just quit the regular Army was hired to help me do the shocking.

This fellow had started in the Army at the time of the Mexican border trouble and had gone all through World War I and then stayed on for an extra stint. He'd been everywhere and seen everything. He was the softest fellow I ever saw and perspired the most. I'm sure he lost 20 pounds in that harvest.

We'd stop every hour or so to rest, and to get a drink from a jug of water wrapped in a wet sack. This fellow would tell us tales of the war and the people he had seen around the world. I'm sure if Aunt Lou had known what he was telling us, there would have been one harvest hand less on the farm before sundown.

After the wheat was shocked we stacked it. In every

farm community there used to be one man who had the ability to stack wheat. Farmers waited their turn for this man for the stacking job. The rest of us hauled bundles to the stack.

Our stacker was an old fellow who liked to make the stacks big, 20 feet across the base and 18 feet high. This meant tossing the heavy bundles high in the air when he was topping out.

Aunt Lou was a wonderful cook, but as we were so far out in the country, we had little fresh meat, unless it would be fried chicken. There was no refrigeration. But we did have a lot of string beans, green and wax, which were coming out of the garden at that time. Aunt Lou cooked them every way she could, often in straight cream. They were good, but a bean is a bean after so many days.

The old stacker was quite a wag. When I was having difficulty tossing a bundle of wheat to him high on the stack, he'd take a moment for a breath and call down:

"Roderick, if you'd just eat one more of those beans, you could get those bundles up here."

This was hard work, but it didn't bother us. At night, we always had something to entertain ourselves. I awakened one night to find Lawrence and the ex-soldier standing by my bed. They had managed to get a little lather on my face and were planning to give me my first shave.

When the weather got real hot, we slept outside. We put hay on an old set of bedsprings and covered this with a sheet. We slept without benefit of pajamas. Here we had to come to an agreement, because at the

155

start there was a race every morning to grab all the clothes and run for the house, leaving one or the other stranded.

It was fair game any time during the night to try to hide the clothes. Sometimes Aunt Lou, who had a big flashlight, would send a beam out across the yard from her bedroom window trying to see what was going on. We'd have to hide behind trees until we could get her to turn the thing off.

We had two ways to get a bath in the evening. One was to fill tubs down behind the barn in the morning. By evening, the water would be lukewarm from the sun. The other was to go to Mission Creek, which ran through the farm, for a swim.

We'd drive to the creek in a buggy pulled by Tom, who doubled as a saddle and buggy horse. The first time, we put our clothes in the buggy while we were in the water, I looked up just in time to see Lawrence hop in the buggy, pop old Tom with the lines and head for home. Only by running fast and cutting across a field was I able to catch up and avoid the necessity of walking nude about a mile to the house.

After that we came to another agreement by which each stashed his clothes equal distance from the buggy.

One night there was a cloudburst and by morning Mission Creek was a river instead of a peaceful little stream. The cows were on the far side of the stream. I had ridden Tom to get the cows but when I saw the flood I turned back to the house for instructions.

Uncle Will said, "You don't need to worry about those cows. They can swim. So can Tom."

"It's your cows and your horse," I said and rode back to the flooded creek. I took off my clothes, hung them on a tree limb, and on old Tom's back, plunged into the muddy water, which was probably 30 feet deep and moving fast. Tom took to it like a duck. The cows were waiting for us on the other side. It took just a little urging and they waddled into the stream. Sure enough, they could swim.

The rain had stopped all farm work for the morning so Lawrence and I took some sticks of dynamite which we had been using to blast old stumps, down to the creek. We'd make a mud ball around the fuse at the point of entrance into the dynamite stick, then light the fuse and throw the thing into the deep water. There'd be a muffled roar and a lot of bubbles would rise to the surface.

After each blast we'd jump into the water as soon as the force of explosion subsided in the hope of gathering in the fish, but we had no luck. Only two or three no-good suckers came to the top. I'm pretty sure dynamiting was against the law even then, but I assume the statute of limitations has long since run out. After all, we didn't get any fish.

Lawrence had a motorcycle. One source of evening entertainment was to ride around a pasture on this vehicle. I sat on the gasoline tank between the handle bars. The grazing horses would take out on a dead run and we'd take out after them.

We also had a mare which we were breaking to ride. She'd throw us every time we got on her back, so we contrived the idea of getting on her in the bed of an old straw stack. She couldn't jump very well in the deep straw and if we fell off, it didn't hurt much.

Culture wasn't entirely overlooked. For instance, Lawrence and I decided we should learn to dance. In fact, one night we rode the motorcycle to Topeka and each spent $1.50 for a dancing lesson.

Thereafter we practiced at noon. Edna would play the organ and as I recall, the tunes were those that she knew—hymns. But she set the metronome for waltz time—one, two, three, one, two, three, one-two-three—while Lawrence and I—both barefoot because we always took our shoes off in the house, would cavort around the carpeted front room floor to "The Little Brown Church in the Wildwood," or some other familiar tune.

The summer went fast, until the harvest ended and dog days set in. My job eventually was to plow wheat land. I'd be in the field all alone, all day, just sitting there on that sulky plow while the horses plodded slowly with their heavy burden.

I got homesick. I persuaded myself that if I were back at Maple Hill, I could get a job with a threshing machine crew at $4 a day and in 10 days make as much as I could working a month on the farm. The next Sunday, I told my father I didn't want to go back.

I've always appreciated his attitude. Stern as he could be at times, he seemed to have a reserve of understanding that came to surface at the proper moment.

Anyone who has been homesick knows how real it can be.

Perhaps my father had been homesick at some time or another. Or maybe I had stayed out on the farm longer than he thought I would in the first place. At any rate, when I announced I was through, he didn't utter a single dissent.

"We'll go get your clothes," he said.

Back home, I did get a job with a threshing crew, but school started before I was able to get in 10 days' work. I was glad to get back to school, too. I had gone that summer from 123 pounds back to 117.

Once Lawrence Romick, then living near Detroit, came through Kansas City and between planes came up to *The Star* office for a short visit. We talked, as you might guess, about one of the best summers either of us ever had, the summer when I worked for his family "by the month" on the farm.

Riding the Caboose

23

THE boredom of Sunday evenings often was relieved by the loading of cattle from the pens on the Rock Island switch track into cars for shipment to market in Kansas City.

Two big ranchers and some small ones were big feeders of cattle at Maple Hill. There were exciting times when the calves were brought in from the ranges by rail to be fed or pastured and again when the fattened animals were loaded out to Kansas City.

The cattle to be shipped out would be driven from feed lots or bluestem pastures down country roads to "stockyards," holding pens along the railroad tracks, by men on horses. Most of these were ranch hands who, for the time being were "cowboys," but the next day they'd be working in hay fields or hauling feed. Often they put on chaps for the occasion. They did have good saddle horses supplied by the ranches.

Driving the cattle into the cars was a noisy event.

The bawling of the animals and the shouts of the cowboys could be heard all over our little town. My mother thought it was a disgrace that such happenings should take place on a Sunday, but I suppose they shipped on Sunday to be on Monday's market—a practice that continues to this day, although they usually move the animals now by truck instead of by train.

Boys of my age enjoyed both the noise and the excitement. We liked to watch the ranch employees, after a car had been loaded, inch it down the tracks with big crowbars under the wheels to make room for another car for a second load. Later on, a freight engine would be seen in the darkness down the tracks and this engine would hook onto the loaded cars to join them in the train that was to take them on the overnight haul to Kansas City.

The loading job done, the cowboys would race their horses down Main street on their way back to the ranch. It was about as near as we ever came to the Old West in Maple Hill. Incidentally, not only did the cowboys not get paid for working overtime; they also weren't paid for working on Sunday. I recall comments that one reason the ranches shipped on Sunday was that they got an extra day's work for nothing.

When the freight trains left Maple Hill, or anywhere else, the last car always was the caboose. I heard as a boy that when a man shipped cattle to market, he could go along on the caboose to watch after them. Also, the railroad would provide him with a free ticket for the trip back home in a passenger train.

I never got to ride a caboose to Kansas City, never

having shipped any cattle, or even helped load them. But often I have thought about the caboose rides and the fellows that made them. And I have visited with some "old-timers" who had many personal recollections of such trips.

One was Cliff Kaney, veteran commission man at the stockyards and one of Kansas City's better-known citizens, Kaney got his first job at the yards when he was 15 years old, in 1907. Moving rapidly from his first job as a messenger to a position as cattle buyer, Kaney recalled going into Nebraska for purchases. He'd help buy and load several carloads of the beef animals, then, along with farmer-owners, ride the caboose back to Kansas City.

Mike Flynn, another veteran commission man, remembered that as a Missouri farm lad of 12 he was allowed to ride the caboose with his father with cattle destined for Chicago.

But for a fellow who actually "lived" an era of the caboose and the livestockman-passengers, there was B. R. Dew, of Des Moines, officially retired as a Rock Island assistant general manager, but who came up through the ranks as a brakeman, conductor and superintendent. His first work as a brakeman was with the Missouri Pacific in Western Kansas. He recalled that he was fascinated by the wide-open spaces, the miles of no trees or water, jack rabbits and coyotes, but most of all by the cattlemen who rode the cabooses and the tall tales they would tell.

The livestockman who rode the caboose was doing a job—it wasn't just a free ride. He had to care for his cattle. At every stop—and Kaney remembered this—

162

the attendant, be he rancher, farmer or just a hired man, was supposed to take a look at his cattle. If one was down, he used a stick he carried to prod him to his feet. He did this day or night.

"Many times it was the owner of the cattle who accompanied them," Dew recalled. "Sometimes it was a son or relative, a cowboy or someone who wanted to see the sights of the big city—which, in our territory, was Kansas City. These men had their chance to get away from home, to see the city lights, the 'girlie shows,' the big bars and hotels. It was a trip they could talk about for years.

"Then, after the cattle were sold," said Dew, "and a few days of looking at the sights, they would pick up their free pass from the railroad agent and head home. I remember on a Sunday night and Monday the old 'Scenic Limited' was crowded with drovers going home, worn out but happy, particularly if the market was good."

As Dew recalled the old caboose, it was kept clean, with plenty of coal and kindling for the stove, a can of drinking water with a long handled tin dipper and a barrel of water for washing up. This barrel, he said, was equipped with a board, or wooden float, so water would not splash out.

"The rear end of a freight train did not ride exactly like a Rolls Royce," he remembered.

"The slack between couplers of 50 and 60 cars on the little 'hog backs' of dips in the track, found many a stockman skating on his back from one end of the caboose to the other, until he learned to sit down and stay set."

163

Dew remembered, too, that some railroads had regular "drovers' cabooses" which were attached just ahead of the regular caboose on the freight. These were equipped with about six upper and lower berths. The uppers pulled down like old Pullman berths. During the days, all mattresses were put on the upper berths and the lowers were used as benches.

The caboose had a desk in one corner and a pull-down table where men could eat and play pitch or poker. There also was a flat-top stove on which coffee was kept hot. Cabooses offered no linens or towels, but occasionally a livestockman would bring his own towel or blanket. And, of course, there was no electricity, just kerosene lamps attached to the wall in each corner. Brakeman, conductor and every livestock attendant had his own coal-oil lantern.

The attendants earned their free ride, Dew said, when they had to get out in the middle of the night and stumble along the tracks in snow, mud and rocks to check their cattle with no light except from the lanterns.

"An old boy once told me," he related, "that a brakeman's lantern made no more light than a 'squirrel waving a lightning bug'."

The brakeman, incidentally, had his own bunk in the cupola of the caboose. That was his domain and the livestockman ventured into it only when invited.

An ordinary caboose would accommodate perhaps as many as eight livestock attendants. Sometimes, these fellows would have box lunches packed by their wives. Other times, they would stop at towns where there'd be a little restaurant near the depot where they could get sandwiches. The railroad crew would be good enough to stop the train so that the caboose would be near the depot. In fact, in most instances, the rapport between the trainmen and the farmers would be good—they were all men working hard for a living.

These were the days, of course, when all livestock moved by train. They were the days of the big terminal markets and the packing centers such as Kansas City, Omaha and Chicago. They began with the extension of the railroads to Dodge City, Wichita, Abilene and other famous livestock centers of the West and ended when the trucks traveling over paved highways took over the bulk of the business.

It was a rugged day and the trip to the city on the caboose was a pleasure only "relative" to the times. The era of the caboose as a host to the cattleman created many stories which are fading from the scene as fewer and fewer of those who went through the experiences remain to tell them.

One story that Dew told concerns hogs.

"Another brakeman and I were loading a car of hogs in a Western Kansas town," the story went. "We got them all in but one old sow; we used clubs, sticks, yells and everything else, besides some choice railroad language, and finally got her headed for the chute. She got part way up and then whirled and came back. My partner saw her coming. So, as it was dark, he jumped in front of her and stuck his lighted lantern between his legs. Well, you know, nothing stops a hog. She weighed about 400 and she hit the old boy with her head down, and brother, both his legs were skinned from knees to ankles."

Another one of Dew's stories was about a lone lad, about 20, who was riding a caboose with Western Kansas cattle heading for Kansas City.

"It was getting daylight, and the sun was coming up on the Kansas plains, bright, which made me drowsy, and I recall I was trying to stay awake. The old conductor—we call him Ed—was a noted prevaricator, harmless, but amusing. The one drover, the lad of 20, was up in the cupola and Old Ed was giving him an example of his folklore. He said:

" 'Son, I was a cowboy in Nebraska years ago. I drove all the cattle out of Western Nebraska on a cattle drive for three seasons. The third year we had a tremendous herd, in fact when the first cow walked into the Platte river, the water was six inches deep, but when the last cow went over, the water was running over her back.'

"I awaked about that time and said, 'Ed, what are you saying?' He answered, 'Boy, there were so many cattle they dammed up the river'."

For another incident, Cliff Kaney remembered a ride in from New Mexico when a cowboy who was tired of sitting on a caboose bench ventured up to the brakeman's bunk in the cupola. The brakeman was gone at the time. But when he returned, he ordered the cowboy out. The cowboy became so angry he kicked down the stove pipe from the stove and then just to show how mad he really was, picked up the stove and threw it out the door.

But most of the time, Kaney recalled, the rides were routine and just "part of the job." Not much money changed hands in the pitch and poker games because few of the men had large amounts of money—going to market. And, it was the practice of commission firms to urge a farmer to take only part of his pay for cattle in cash—it would be better, he would be advised, to have the remainder mailed to his bank at home.

Some of the card sharks might get it all, Kaney explained.

What did the livestockmen do when they got to Kansas City?

Most of them headed for a hotel or restaurant to get something to eat. The stockyards area was "wide-open" all night, Kaney recalled—restaurants, bars and hotels. A man could get a good meal for a quarter, or a plate of beans, crackers and a cup of coffee for a dime.

Stories abound about the wild experiences of the livestockmen "painting the town," and many were true. But Kaney insisted most of the visitors had worked too hard for the little cash they received to throw it away. Not all, but most of them, got their free tickets for the ride home and took their money back to their families.

One more incident! Kaney recalled when he first saw a motor truck deliver a cow to the stockyards. An old-timer, sitting in front of a saloon, also viewing the scene, commented:

"I never thought I'd live to see the day when a cow got a ride in a hack."

In case you don't remember what a hack was, it was a horse-drawn taxicab.

First Long Pants

THE excitement that accompanies the acquisition of an entire new wardrobe by the modern pupil going back to school still does not match that surrounding the boy who wore his first pair of long pants as he returned to the country school.

In Maple Hill this event usually took place when a boy entered high school and it was a new mark of distinction. To the boy it meant he began to regard himself as a man. To others, it signified that from now on he would be classified among the "big boys" at school, rather than the little fellows.

When a boy appeared in his new long pants, the older folks would make comments such as "My, how these boys do grow up nowadays; I well remember the day he was born and look at him now in those long pants looking just like a man. Takes after his father, too."

The older high school girls tended to be complimentary.

I can remember it was the Carlson girls, sisters of my school mate, John Carlson, who told me I looked just fine. Wearing my new trousers, I had casually walked down to see John. The trousers were part of a dark green tweed suit. Of course, I didn't wear the new suit to school, but along with this suit I had bought a pair of school trousers.

Part of the joy of getting long trousers was in outliving the short pants that were in vogue in that day. These pants came to just below the knee. There was a strap with a buckle that was supposed to hold the pants in place, but this never worked, even when the buckle wasn't torn loose.

Also, these pants were made with sort of a universal waist size. Those of us who were skinny and without a hip line always were trying to get our belts tight enough to hold our pants up.

We, of course, had no tailors in Maple Hill to alter the waist lines. Our mothers all sewed, but they were not able to tailor a pair of boys pants.

Long pants also meant graduation from long black stockings which went with the short-pants costume. These stockings were the bane of a boy's existence.

In the first place, holes constantly appeared in either the heel or the knee.

"I just can't keep you boys in stockings," my mother used to wail. And it was a chore. She had a small gourd which she thrust into the stockings while she darned them. A poorly darned sock could cause irritation.

There was a time when a mail order house offered

169

stocking feet for sale. The old foot would be cut from the stocking at the ankle and the new foot sewed on. But they never fit right and the seam at the ankle always was visible.

Even worse than the long stockings were the garters that had to be worn to keep them up. Our mother made these from either white or black elastic she bought at the store. The garters never felt comfortable, they were forever losing their stretch and they had a habit of being lost just when you had to have them most on a Sunday morning.

No wonder it was a great event when a boy became a "man" and got his first long pants. It was a graduation into a new era.

Put it down as a mark in progress when the short pants with the fastener at the knee were discarded forever. This step came shortly after I finished school. In speaking of the good old days, I don't think any man ever refers to short pants or long stockings. But I wonder what thrill has taken its place as a lad moves from the small boy category into the world of big boys.

As I recall, there really wasn't much of a flurry around our house late in summer about getting clothes ready for school. Our parents perhaps were more concerned than us boys. I don't recall paying any attention to the advertisements on school clothes. We could get our clothes in two ways—either by driving to Topeka or ordering from Montgomery Ward and Sears Roebuck.

For our good suits, we usually went to the Palace in Topeka, where Orson Baker, a former Maple Hill boy, was a clerk in the men's clothing department. Mr. Baker, who was as old as my father, or older, always liked to tell that he had been born in a cabin between Maple Hill and Topeka. The site now is at an intersection on I-70 west of Topeka. This is the story he told:

The time of the birth was near when a heavy snowstorm engulfed the area. His father took a team and headed for Topeka to get a doctor while an older brother started on foot on the same quest to Dover, the nearest town.

Because of the heavy snow, it was two days before either was able to return. By that time, the baby had been born and neighboring farm women had taken care of things. Baker always claimed that he was sitting up in bed laughing when his dad and brother arrived back at the house.

We always thought Baker would see that we got a good deal on our clothes and we did.

In grade school, the boys usually wore either short pants or overalls. In high school, we were a little dressier and usually wore long pants that would be classified somewhere between work gear and good clothes. Incidentally, we had no such things as jeans.

In our school the high school boys polished their shoes; maybe it was just a fad, but we prided ourselves on the shine that was evident at least when we walked into school in the mornings.

We made our own football shoes; that is we had cleats put on ordinary shoes. It was only with reluctance that our school board would finance the purchase of a new football each year. Such other equip-

171

ment as we had we purchased ourselves.

For playing shoes, we would buy a pair of cheap work shoes with low uppers. Then we'd have the local cobbler nail pieces of sole leather onto the shoe sole as cleats. As I recall, the system worked. Regular football shoes, we assumed, were for college players only.

No boy in our school had an overcoat. We believed that possessing such a coat indicated that the young man was a sissy. However, I'm sure the attitude developed from the fact nobody expected to get such a coat.

We went through a series of fads on sweaters. First there was the heavy wool pullover sweater with a big roll at the neck. Then there was a finer wool sweater, also a pullover type. Put on enough shirts under these sweaters and you didn't need an overcoat. Also, with the sweaters—and no coat—your arms were free for play.

When winter approached, our mother always ordered from either Montgomery Ward or Sears two pairs of long underwear for each of us boys. We changed every Saturday night.

Even in school there were days when the old furnace just wouldn't get the rooms warm. The teacher would interrupt the classes to have us all stand for exercises to get us warm. Obviously, with the slightest indication of an unduly cool room, we'd show signs of discomfort and the need for the exercise.

Long underwear certainly had a place back in those days when homes were not heated at night and the motor cars were the touring models open at all sides. Here again, however, is one part of the good old days that I think people are glad to leave behind.

The best thing that came along for our group was the mackinaw, a heavy short coat. The farm boys were the first to acquire these. These coats had big collars which could be pulled up as protection against the wind. They abetted the caps with the genuine skunk fur earflaps that we all wore in the winter to keep our ears warm.

Looking back, we just didn't require a very extensive wardrobe for school, so no wonder we were not overly interested in the fall styles. However, I would not want to give the impression that we were poorly clad. We all had what we wanted and needed.

And the girls? There was none in our family so I have no knowledge of school preparations. I do recall the most common and universal costume was the white middy blouse with blue tie and the blue wool skirt. I don't recall that any girl ever won a beauty contest in one of these outfits. Fortunately, they had other clothes which may not have been so practical, but were far prettier.

One fad took over our school at about the time I was in the eighth grade. It was the pompadour hair style for boys. From eighth grade on up, all the boys took to wearing the top of one of our mother's stockings on our heads as we slept. In the morning, our hair would be slicked back. With the addition of a coating of hair cream and frequent combings throughout the day, it would stay slicked back.

There was a movie guy named Valentino who set the pace.

Walnuts, Food and Fun

25

THE first sharp frost of the fall season was the signal for walnut gathering time in our home town.

Much earlier we had spotted the trees in the woods along Mill Creek, Dry Creek and adjacent to the Kaw River which had the best crops. When frost dropped the walnuts to the ground, we were ready for them.

This was before walnuts were worth money. Harold Gallaher, extension forester at Kansas State University, reports mechanical walnut hullers have been placed at several locations in the state by companies which buy the nuts for commercial use. Prices, he says, are expected to be about $2.50 a hundred pounds for unhulled walnuts and $3 for the hulled ones.

At those prices many of us boys in Maple Hill were rich in inventory and didn't know it. However, for us gathering walnuts was something of a picnic and eating the delicious kernels was glorious pastime.

We liked to gather walnuts where they were thick. There was, for instance, one big tree along Dry Creek on the Sells ranch which stood at the edge of a little ditch. The ditch was narrow and deep, carved out of the soil by water running off a wheat field.

Walnuts from the tree fell into the ditch and this really was hitting the jackpot. All you had to do was hold a gunny sack open and roll them in. The fact was, you could get all you wanted in a few minutes. But we never stopped with just enough. We filled sack after sack to create a big pile in the back yard at home.

Once upon a time there were trees along the road south of town at Tod's cattle feeding corrals. You could get all the walnuts you'd want from the roadside, but this was too easy. We boys chose to go farther back into the woods. Those trees are gone now.

Lawrence Romick, who lived on a farm close to town, rigged up a regular cart to haul walnuts. It was a big box on an old buggy chassis. Lawrence (nicknamed Nunks, which was short for skunk, because so often in the winter his cotton gloves carried the skunk odor) had a horse named Dick.

Lawrence and I hitched up Old Dick to the cart one fine late October Saturday to gather walnuts along Mill Creek. Somehow the walnuts on the other side of the creek appeared more plentiful, larger or better. Anyway, we had to drive the cart across the creek at some riffles. Coming back, with the cart loaded, the nondescript tugs came loose and Old Dick went on, leaving us and the cart stranded in the middle of the stream. Dick stopped on shore and patiently waited.

This was a delightful predicament. We promptly

took off our clothes, waded across to where Dick was standing, took him back and hooked up to the cart again. It is pretty hard to have excitement gathering walnuts, but we accomplished the feat.

Some trees had better walnuts than others. There was one just below Hamilton's falls on Mill Creek which always produced nuts of excellent quality. Since this tree was on the route we usually took on rabbit and squirrel hunts in the Buffalo Mound area, we often stopped under its bare branches for a lunch—of walnuts. We carried salt in the watch pockets of our overalls. Salt was good on walnut kernels. We also had our pockets crammed with apples. Salted walnut meats and apples will carry you a long way.

The walnuts under this Mill Creek tree were available all winter as it was far off the beaten path and no one picked them up to take them home. We used rocks to crack the hard shells.

One cold winter day when the creek was frozen we decided to vary our diet. We had killed a rabbit and decided to barbecue it. We skinned it, cut a hole in the ice and soused the rabbit up and down in the cold water to get the carcass clean. Then we hung it on a stick over a fire. All I can report is that burned rabbit meat isn't good.

Gathering walnuts can be a family affair. When we got our first car, we'd drive to the woods, carry our empty sacks to the trees, and drag the full sacks back to the car. Since cars then had no trunks, we piled the sacks on the fenders, and in the back seat. Not quite as good as a wagon, but quicker.

Gathering walnuts was fun, but hulling them was a

different matter. An old corn sheller would do a pretty good job. Easier to find was a board with a knot hole, We'd lay the board on two rocks, then drive the green walnuts through the hole. The hull, of course, would be knocked off in the process. This went on until we had plenty of walnuts for immediate eating. The remainder we just left in the pile in the back yard. Eventually they dried and the hulls cracked off.

The walnut pile was a meeting place after school, early in the evenings. We'd crack and eat them by the hour. Although rich, the walnut meats apparently wouldn't hurt the digestive system if you had to crack and pick them out as you went along.

We had all heard the story of one boy who had grown up in Maple Hill and who got sick eating walnuts. This was the late Ed Chapman. Ed had a desire to eat all he wanted at one sitting without having to stop to crack them. So, he cracked and picked out a full tincup of walnut kernels. Then he proceeded to consume them. He nearly died.

So we ate ours one kernel at a time, adding a little salt to tease the appetite.

We did, however, occasionally pick out the kernels by the cupsful. The high school girls would offer to make fudge if we would furnish the walnut kernels. This was a perfect combination. They'd sit with us and watch us as we cracked the walnuts. Then we'd watch them make the fudge. Then we'd all eat it.

It was an evening's entertainment at almost no cost. This was good, because as mentioned earlier, we didn't gather walnuts for money and looked upon them only as one of nature's contributions to happy living.

Huntin' Dogs

26

FOR sheer excitement in the
world of boyhood, I can think of nothing that exceeds
watching a dog or two trying to dig a rabbit, 'possum
or 'coon from its den in the ground.

At least that is the way it was when the boys at
Maple Hill used to hunt with dogs in the woods along
Mill Creek or in the deep ravines of the bluestem
covered Flint Hills that surrounded the town.

Nothing works with more fury or enthusiasm than a
dog that thinks he has a quarry cornered deep in a
hole, especially when he is cheered on by human
hunting pals. His front paws tear at the dirt, throwing
it out in a spray between his hind feet. His ferocious
growl tells the world he is aiming for bear.

In such situations, we could stand by hollering "sick
'em, go git him." Or we'd attempt, as we pushed the
dog aside, to reach into the hole with a forked stick to
see if we could locate the prey. If there were more than

one dog on the hunt—and we usually had several—they'd take turns digging. Sometimes two would get their heads and front feet into the hole, both churning earth furiously. You would get covered with dirt if you stood behind them. It was a time to jump up and down and cheer.

We had a variety of dogs that fit all purposes. My middle brother, Bernard, and I had a bird dog named "Snap."

He got that name from a previous dog called Snap owned by our grandfather. That Snap had been killed by a mean and bigger dog. We had wanted a replacement.

One day I was standing in the door of our blacksmith shop in Maple Hill when a mother bird dog strolled down the street trailed by a brood of puppies. I was pretty small, because I barely remember the occasion, but my father often related the events that followed so I know what happened.

I looked the pups over, and my eye set upon a white pup with liver spots. I picked him up in my arms and announced to my father that:

"This one is mine."

"Now wait a minute," my father commented as he smiled to some farmers standing in the shop. "You just can't take a pup like that. You'll have to ask Jim Pete to see if he'll let you have him."

Jim Pete was Jim Clark, who ran the telephone office, worked and farmed around Maple Hill and also loved to hunt and fish. Such men usually are kind hearted.

I started home with my new pup in my arms.

179

"His name is Snap," I said.

"You've got to ask Jim Pete first," my father admonished again.

By this time Clark had joined the group at the shop.

"I guess there's nothing much I can do," he said with a grin, and I walked on home to meet my next challenge—whether mother would let me keep the pup.

It seems that I won out because we had Snap for a long time.

Of course I never had papers that would prove Snap was a purebred, but I heard that he was a real bird dog. Even when he was a spindle-legged pup, he would chase sparrows or anything else with feathers.

Without the least bit of training, Snap would point quail. In fact, he'd point anything alive, including rabbits. And since we were not interested in quail alone, it just goes to show how smart he was for the company he was keeping.

Fact is, when we were real young, we hunted with dogs alone because our folks wouldn't let us have guns. After we had grown up some, perhaps to 10 years, we began to get single shot .22s, 410s, or even 12-gauge single barrel guns, none of which are too effective on quail.

Our hunts were more of an adventure than a quest for game. We went out for rabbits, mostly, also 'possums, squirrels, civet cats or skunks. We always hoped that someday we would find a raccoon.

So in our sorties with our dogs, every hole in the ground, every nest in a tree, every brush pile was in a fortress that might hold some wild animal. We tore into them with gusto.

Some of the best dens were along the banks of Mill Creek. Under the roots of big trees were all kinds of holes leading into mysterious caverns deep into the soil. The dogs would bite at the roots and tear into the soil with their paws seeking to get back into the dark passages where presumably a rabbit or 'possum crouched in a remote corner.

I'll have to admit that most of the time, we never got back to the end of the "den." Though the dirt flew and the dog growled, headway was difficult. The animals apparently were smart enough most of the time to pick deep holes.

Even when we did get to the den nest, we'd find it empty. Apparently the dogs, led on by scent, were digging just in hope.

Brush piles were particular targets. With the dogs barking fiercely and tense with excitement, two or three of us boys would get on top the pile and start jumping up and down. If there was a rabbit present, after so much commotion, he would decide to make a run for it.

Yelping, the dogs would frantically take off in pursuit.

Likely as not the rabbit would seek haven in another brush pile, and we'd have the same process to repeat. It took lots of jumping to get rabbits out of brush piles.

Our dogs were just dogs, but they were rugged. Smart, too.

Out-Sitting the Squirrel

27

RAY Heady, *The Star's* outdoor editor once lamented a dearth of interest in squirrel hunting which he attributed to a lack of patience. Hunters today, he said, just won't take the time necessary to "sit out" the squirrels high up in the trees.

Well, Ray was right. It does take patience, and we boys learned that. It didn't come naturally, because by nature we were rambunctious hunters. Ordinarily we took as many dogs as would tag along with us, we jumped on every brush pile, poked sticks into holes under trees, shook the grapevines tangled around limbs which held squirrel nests, and cheered the dogs whenever they thought they had found something in a hole in the creek bank.

Of course, we were hunting for any animal that roamed the fields or woods—squirrels, rabbits, 'possums, 'coons, skunks or civet cats.

It was exciting when the dogs concluded they had something down a hole and would furiously seek to dig it out.

The dirt would literally fly and the dogs would whine with impatience as they tore with their front paws into the underground den. Often as not we'd end up with nothing more than a field mouse, or maybe the tunnel would take a turn and the bottom of the hole would be in China as far as we ever would know.

But once in awhile we struck pay dirt. There was the time on the big hill west of town when, after the dogs had dug for a spell, we lay down flat and looked into the hole. For sure there was something there—two beady eyes. So we sicked the dogs into digging some more.

The beady eyes, it turned out, belonged to a big, broad-stripe, prairie skunk. When the dogs pulled him out, we ran. There was a brief, but smelly fight. The dogs didn't even like themselves for several days.

But back to squirrels. The fount of all hunting knowledge in our town was the barbershop. Jack Herron, the barber, was an expert hunter. We boys regarded him with awe.

In the first place, he had the kind of equipment we wished for. He had a canvas hunting coat in which he could carry game. He had a regular hunter's cap. More than that, he had a .22 repeater, a double-barrel 20-gauge, a 12-gauge pump and an Army rifle. Most of us boys were lucky to have either a single-barrel shotgun or .22.

Just before and during World War I, our town had a small group which went under the name of the Home

Guard, or some other appropriate title. The few men in this group, including Jack Herron, had Army rifles and put up a target in a draw west of town. They could stand at the edge of town and shoot at the target more than a quarter a mile away.

One day a big flock of geese flew over town. Jack, whose home was in the north part of town, aimed his Army rifle carefully at the leading point of the V and fired. A big goose dropped out of the sky and landed on the school's football field at the south end of town. I'm telling you it would have been too bad for any German airplane that flew over our town in that war.

The barber shop was the place where local hunters gathered to talk about their exploits. We boys naturally liked to listen. My brother, Bernard, Bill Clements, John Carlson and myself were there late one Saturday afternoon, just sitting. We had been hunting squirrels most of the day.

Jack had a customer in the chair getting his Saturday shave. He stopped a moment to strop his razor and inquired if we boys had had any luck. We told him no, we hadn't seen a single squirrel.

"I'll bet a lot of them saw you," Jack commented. The men in the barber shop joined him in laughing at this observation.

"How come?" we asked.

Jack took the time to explain to us that squirrels can hear you coming. The way to hunt them, he said, is to walk quietly and then sit down some place. The squirrels see you and hide, but they can stay put only so long. First thing you know, one of them will move his head or his tail and then you locate him.

184

We found out Jack was as right as he could be. Old Doc Taylor, farmer south of town, had a patch of woods on Dry Creek, adjacent to a corn field. The squirrels from the woods ate a lot of Doc's corn. He invited us out to hunt them. We found that if we'd go out early in the morning, sit down quietly on a stump and wait, sure enough we'd see the squirrels hopping from the corn back to the woods.

The squirrels favored big, tall cottonwoods along Mill Creek. We would surround such trees, lie down and wait, constantly scanning the limbs for that tell-tale movement that would mark our quarry.

One afternoon John Carlson and I were hunting with a woefully small amount of ammunition. In fact, John had two cartridges for his single-shot Stevens .22. I had about six for my Remington. We had to make our own money to buy shells and our best source was the sale of rabbit or squirrel meat.

A squirrel freshly dressed, would bring 20 cents. A box of 50 cartridges cost 15 cents. To get back into business, each of us had to kill a squirrel that afternoon.

Luckily, I got my squirrel first, so it was John's turn. We focused our attention on a huge cottonwood on the creek bank that leaned just a little toward the creek, which was deep at that point. Sure enough, after a bit of patience, we spied a red tail twitching high on a limb. This squirrel was smart. He got on the creek side of the tree. I began to move around to attract his attention while John stationed himself at the base of the tree, at the edge of the creek. By looking straight up the tree he could see his target. He took careful aim at his quarry and fired.

The squirrel dropped into the creek.

We had to have that squirrel. With the aid of a dead limb we soon "fished" him ashore.

With one squirrel each, we headed for home. We seldom "made a killing." Perhaps two or three squirrels, sometimes five or six rabbits. We counted the fun more than the meat. Not only that, what we killed, we carried home. Five or six rabbits hanging from your belt is a heavy load if you have two or three miles to walk. And the trip home was always at the end of the day when you were tired out.

We were in our glory in winters with heavy snow. Since our main sport was hunting, the snow was an asset. You could tell from the tracks where the rabbits were. But more than that, the snow created a new world to explore. This is something hard to describe, because as boys we didn't think of it exactly in that way, but I know now it was true. You could climb to the top of a hill and look at an entirely new landscape. This was adventure.

Big drifts along draws were our favorite havens. We would jump into them. If the snow were soft enough, we would sink clear out of sight. Or, we would dig a hole and, along with the dogs, crawl in out of the wind, imagining that we were getting a respite from the cold. We would dig into old straw stacks to escape the bitter winds.

Magically, however, warmth returned whenever we made a good shot and got our rabbit. We used to wonder about this and comment on whether the excitement of shooting straight made our blood run faster or whether it just warmed up from walking.

The big thrill came each fall when we were out in the old river bed, late in the afternoon, on the day of the first cold wave. Then the first flight of ducks came in. To be honest, we had single-shot guns and we didn't get many ducks. But we liked to be out by the river when the flight began. It would be a cold, raw evening with a little mist or perhaps a few snowflakes falling. The clouds would be low and we couldn't see too far. It would be just a little bit eerie and we would be sort of expecting something to happen.

Then we would peer off into the misty distance and see them coming, a big flock silently cutting a pathway just beneath the clouds. In a moment they would be out of sight. Then we would see another and another, too high for the gun, yet low enough that we knew they were looking for a place to land for the night.

Temptation would be great and as the flock went directly overhead we would point our gun skyward and fire. There would be a cry from the leader as his companions broke their V and bunched, putting on a new burst of speed and disappearing into the mist.

Our chances of getting ducks that night were gone. Who cared? We knew that the next morning we could sneak up on a patch of water in the old river bed and get the shot that would count. It would be a cold, early morning walk out to that old river. Of course we didn't have to go. We could stay in bed. There would be more ducks later.

The Old Stone Fence

28

In my mind, nothing is more intriguing to a boy hunter and his dogs than an old stone fence. We had such a fence on a side hill near Maple Hill.

The fence was about three miles from town on "the other side" of Buffalo Mound, the biggest hill in the area and one of the highest in Kansas' famous Flint Hills. The location of the fence was an isolated one, far out in the open spaces and along an old trail. It brought up vestiges of pioneer days to us boys who probed in its rough fabric in search of rabbits.

I never knew who built the fence or even why, because it wasn't serving to keep cattle either in or out the quarter mile of its length along the ridge of the hill. Doubtless there had been a reason at some time. Stone was used for the fence because there was plenty of it laying loose on the rocky hillside.

By our time the fence had been abandoned as to

utility, the stones were toppling. We boys helped the deterioration when our dogs by their yelping indicated a rabbit hidden in some inner recess.

The main attribute of the fence was, of course, that it was a haven for rabbits.

Just getting to the fence from town was an adventure, although we didn't dignify it with any such term as we set out from our homes, our pockets filled with apples, shotgun shells, cotton gloves and pocket knives that had been sharpened on a whetstone at the blacksmith shop.

John Carlson, my brother, Bernard (a second brother, Don, was too young), and I headed first for the railroad tracks. Running ahead were our dogs, Snap, a birddog that pointed rabbits, much to our delight, and John's dogs, a big shepherd and a little rat terrier. Some other dogs of the neighborhood might tag along.

Reaching the tracks, we would walk the rails, vying with each other to see who could tread the narrow band of steel the longest before slipping off. When a Rock Island train was seen coming, we would move to the side of the tracks to get the benefit of the cloud of smoke that poured from the steam engine, imagining, at least, that the smoke carried some warmth with it. Anyway, it was fun being hidden for a few moments in the black cloud.

We'd leave the tracks to cross the slough on Uncle Al Romick's farm. The slough, a mass of heavy grass, would be crossed and criss-crossed with rabbit and muskrat trails. The dogs would go wild on these trails, but seldom could they stir the rabbits from their hideouts. Even if they did, the cottontails would scurry to grass cover again before we could shoot. The slough looked like a wonderful place to hunt, but, from experience, we knew it was of little use to linger too long.

So we headed on across an alfalfa field for Mill Creek. If the creek were frozen solid, we crossed on the ice. But more often, we would make our crossing at Hamilton's Falls.

Hamilton's Falls was a place on Mill creek on Walt Hamilton's farm where the creek bottom changed. For miles above, the water was deep, the bottom of the creek either gravel or mud. But just above what was called the Falls, the bottom was a layer of solid rock. This layer was broken and then continued as another layer at a lower level. The water gushed over these broken rocks at a rapid rate (and still does) for about three quarters of a mile to even larger "falls" at Rocky Ford on Steel Romick's farm below.

Crossing Hamilton's Falls involved jumping from one rock to another. We always were able to make it, but not always without getting wet feet. The dogs, of course, had no trouble.

On the other side of the creek was a ravine. By following the ravine, we came upon a spring hidden beneath a small cliff. Even in coldest weather, the spring would be running, forming a small pool of beautifully clear water about two feet deep, and some six or seven feet across.

Sometimes the pool would be frozen over and covered with ice and snow, with only the flow of water from the spring shoing as it disappeared under the winter canopy. We threw heavy rocks onto the ice in an effort to break it.

Beyond the spring was rolling bluestem prairie, the pathway to Buffalo Mound. And then, just south of the mound and below it, was the old stone fence.

The fence was on a south slope, protected from the north wind. Beyond the fence was a gully where there had been an old wagon trail. The route, even then was known as the Tenth Street Road, because it was directly west of Tenth Street in Topeka, 21 miles east. At some time it had been a wagon route from Topeka to Ft. Riley. It didn't deserve the dignity of the word "road" anymore. It served better as good rabbit-hunting territory.

South of the gully and fence was a limitless stretch of bluestem prairie pasture.

We hunted by walking along the old stone fence, letting the dogs investigate every hole between the rocks. The rabbits, stirred from their warm hovels, almost inevitably scampered down the gully. And, with our old single-barrel shotguns, we'd blast away.

When there was snow on the ground, the rabbit tracks would be thick around the old fence. With this evidence, we were almost certain we'd find game.

The actual hunt would last half an hour or perhaps three-quarters. Seldom were we disappointed, particularly if the wind was in the north. We'd get four, five, sometimes even six or seven cottontails.

Then came the long walk back home, to be enlivened, we'd hope, with a a shot or two at a speedy jackrabbit.

The old stone fence is gone. In fact, I'm not sure I

191

could locate just where it used to be, unless I followed the same route we used to take as boys.

Interstate No. 70, a fine four-lane highway, now cuts through the south side of Buffalo Mound. It is on the old Tenth Street Road route. I think the "cut" for the new highway was made exactly where the gully below the fence used to be.

I travel the road often and enjoy its smooth magnificence, but I never pass Buffalo Mound without a tinge of nostalgia for the old stone fence.

Incidentally, travelers heading west out of Topeka on I-70 first get a glimpse of Buffalo Mound about eight miles out of the capital city. It looms in the distance like a Rocky mountain from the East Colorado plains, but loses its stature as the highway in a gentle slope actually cuts through the side of the hill.

Candidates
Were Safe in Maple Hill

29

A RECENT political campaign was marked by heckling of the candidates when they tried to speak, and on occasion, things were thrown at them. Stones and other objects narrowly missed the presidential candidates.

I am glad the inclination to stone candidates did not prevail when I was a boy because if we had thrown, we would have hit. Somebody might have been hurt.

I don't want to suggest that we were sharpshooters or anything like that. We couldn't equal those stories we used to hear from the Ozarks about boys who not only killed squirrels with rocks, but always hit them in the head so that the would not damage the carcass. But the fact was, we were throwing at something a good part of the time and we were in "practice." We couldn't hit a squirrel, but we were pretty good on larger targets.

We started playing baseball at Maple Hill when we

were in the first grade. There were four boys in my first grade class and our wonderful teacher, Miss Cora Jacobs, gave us time after each recess to relate to her a play-by-play account of the "one-old cat" game we had had during that interval in our studies.

Baseball was a main part of our recreation throughout school. Being a little town school, we didn't have a large number of boys in any age group, so, in order to have a game, everybody had to play. Our favorite game we called "work up" and it was simply a process of working yourself up from right field to batter. When you made an out as a batter, you went back to right field and had to play back to catcher before you were at bat again. In this process, every boy at certain intervals was the pitcher.

When we were not actually engaged in a game, we were playing "catch." Since we usually had only one catcher's mitt in our school, several of us would pitch to the lone catcher.

This went on before school, at recesses and after school. It was a favorite pastime Saturdays and Sundays.

In the summer I almost always could get up a game of catch with two or three boys who would have sauntered down town just to loaf or find something to do.

My brother, Bernard, and I hurried through supper and helping with the dishes (we had no sisters so the dishes were a chore forced on us) in order to play catch until darkness set in. We'd trade off, one pitching awhile and then the other. Each had his way of throwing his fast ball, a drop, an in or an out curve. We

195

thought we were pretty good at the game.

I had my own way of practicing my straight, fast throw. I would prop the clothesline pole up under the wire line and then, at the usual distance from the mound to the catcher, I'd try to knock the pole down. Quite often I did it. My folks used to warn me, "Don't you ever throw at anybody."

But our throwing wasn't confined to baseball. When the town graveled the streets, gravel from Mill Creek was used. This was the grandest supply of throwing rocks that could be imagined. We could stand in the road in front of our house and throw rocks across Updegraff's pasture through the window in the shed at the back of their barn.

Apparently, there was nothing in the shed because while I recollect often putting a rock through the window (there was no glass in it) I don't remember any cow, horse or chicken being provoked to run out the main door.

Another inexhaustible supply of rocks of throwing size was the ballast along the Rock Island railroad tracks. For numerous reasons, such as going out to the hills to hunt, Mill Creek to fish or swim, or just walking, frequently groups of us boys sauntered down the railroad tracks. A favorite pastime was seeing how far you could walk on a rail without falling off.

But with rocks at hand everywhere, a walk along the tracks meant almost constant throwing at things—at fence posts along the right of way, at the myriads of red-winged blackbirds swarming in the slough grass over the fences, and, I think it can be confessed at this late date, we also occasionally smashed a green glass insulator on the telegraph poles.

Some of the rocks used for ballast along the railroad tracks were sandstones. These usually were almost round and about the size of a fist. Such stones thrown hard onto a rail would smash into sand.

From the bridges over Mill Creek, we could throw rocks at the mud turtles sunning themselves on driftwood in the stream below. A near hit would cause the turtle to slip swiftly into the water—can't recall that we ever actually hit one.

We could, occasionally, hit a tin can we had thrown into the water. We would throw at it frantically as it floated down the stream and out of distance. If you hit it, of course, you sank it. It was no mean accomplishment.

It was fun, too, to throw "skippers" in the creek. For this we used a small, flat rock and these were plentiful in the gravel bars along the riffles. Usually, below each riffle was a stretch of deep water. This was an excellent place to throw the skippers and if you were real good, you would make a rock "walk" entirely across the creek.

This meant throwing the flat rock with such force that it would skip across the water, touching the surface at frequent intervals. The trick was to throw the rock so that it landed flat on the water rather than being driven into it.

A walk down any country road meant throwing rocks or clods at telephone poles or at birds sitting on the telephone lines. We could hit the poles occasionally but I don't recall ever being so good as to hit a bird. Maybe they could see the rocks coming.

John Carlson once did hit a bird with his sling shot. This was another way we had of throwing at things. For our sling shots, we cut forked sticks from trees, always keeping an eye out for a fork that was of ideal proportions. We used rubber from old inner tubes in a day when tubes were made of actual rubber and were full of stretch. For the leather that held the ammunition, we cut pieces from old shoes.

The point is that with so much throwing, we boys at Maple Hill would have been capable candidates for any kind of rioting that could have called for pelting a speaker. However, such things never entered our minds.

It seems to me now that most of the candidates who were running for office in our county (Wabaunsee) were seeking the sheriff's post. Their pictures or cards would be tacked onto a board hanging on the blacksmith shop wall along with announcements of farm sales and jacks and stallions standing at stud.

Candidates used to drop into the blacksmith shop, shake hands with my father and ask that he vote for them. Usually, there'd be no more than two or three others (farmers) in the shop at the time. My father would greet the candidate respectfully and tell him honestly whether he would get his vote or whether he already had promised it to someone else. It was a personal matter.

Sen. Charles Curtis, later to become vice-president when Hoover was President, called at Maple Hill once and made a hit with my Uncle Al Romick. Uncle Al had met him once before. On this particular visit,

Senator Curtis inquired of Uncle Al how his sons Jack, Elmer, Murphy and Tom and daughter, Margaret, were getting along. Uncle Al was so proud that a senator had remembered the names of all his family that he was a fan of Curtis's almost the rest of his life.

His allegiance wavered, however, when Curtis allied himself with Hoover, the man who put a ceiling on wheat prices during World War I. Here was the one chance that farmers had to get fantastic supply and demand prices and Hoover ruined it. Uncle Al never forgave him.

But he didn't throw any rocks. None of us did. A candidate would have been safe in Maple Hill.

The First Armistice Day

30

THE almost incredible and sincere joy that swept across the nation at the end of World War I November 11, 1918, was expressed in our little town of Maple Hill in every way we knew how.

The celebration, of course, was spontaneous because it would not have been possible under the circumstances to have planned it.

November 11 that year dawned clear in Maple Hill, a cool, crisp fall morning. The telephone at our house rang just at day break—it was a long distance call from Kansas City and that of course meant something serious we were certain. People didn't put in a long distance call at that time of the day unless they had important news.

This was news—big news. At the other end of the line when my father answered was my uncle, E. B. Chapman, then working on the city desk of *The Star*.

200

The war was over! The armistice had been signed!

Our father shouted the news upstairs where my brothers and mother were still in bed. My brother, Don, was still a little fellow, but my second brother, Bernard, and I hit the floor on the run. We put on trousers and headed for the old Methodist church just across the corner from our house. The church no longer was being used for services, but it did have a bell.

We yanked on the rope and the bell began to toll. In Maple Hill, that meant just one thing—fire.

Down the street we could see Billie Cox coming on the run from his home on another corner. Billie, a short heavy set man, was trying to run, pull on his trousers and get his suspenders over his shoulders all at the same time.

"Where's the fire? Where's the fire?" he shouted breathlessly.

Bernard stuck his head out the church door with the news:

"There isn't any fire, the war is over."

"Aw hell," Billie exclaimed. Only some one who has been called out of his sleep to answer a fire alarm in a little town can appreciate the immediate let down he experienced. However, it was shortlived.

Bernard and I continued to yank on the bell rope. Maybe other folks got telephone calls, too. Anyway, by the time the school yard was filled with youngsters at 8:30, the whole countryside knew that World War I was history.

We decided we wouldn't go to school that day—by acclamation it was a holiday. The principal gathered us together to explain that an impromptu holiday was illegal. He threatened dire punishment, even expulsion of the whole student body. We just laughed and walked away. And I'm sure his conscience was clear because he had tried.

November was the beginning of the hunting season and most of us boys regarded Saturdays, Sundays and holidays as set aside for the particular purpose of the quest for rabbits and squirrels. So, with nothing else planned, we went home and got our shotguns. Actually, we just felt like creating the kind of noise that only a gun could make.

Gathered back on the school grounds, we started shooting at tin cans and Joe McClelland took a long distance shot at the window in the cupola that topped our two-story school house. It was a four-room building that then housed both the grade and high school.

We could hear the shot ping against the glass and we laughed in defiance at the school where the principal tried to get us into classes on the day when THE WAR WAS OVER.

A group of boys meandered down to the slough on a farm south of town. The slough, which had long since been dry from a hot summer, was grown high with grass. It should have been just full of rabbits. But it wasn't. At least we couldn't get any to run where we could see them. From one end of the slough to the other we trampled through the heavy growth. But who cared? We didn't want rabbits anyway. We were celebrating. We shot at field mice or anything else that moved.

By noon, we not only had run out of anything at

which to shoot, but we also were hungry. Some of the farm boys went home as did those of us who lived in town. But the word got around there would be a hot time in town that night.

"Be down on Main street just as soon as supper is over" was the information spread around. And sure enough, most everybody was there. The business block in Maple Hill, incidentally, was just one block long.

But what to do?

Our town never had celebrated the end of the war before. We weren't enough to have a parade—if we had had a parade who would have watched?

There was a fever that had to be squelched someway. Looking back, it is difficult to describe the elation all of us felt. For some of the older folks, it meant sons were coming home. For us boys it meant older brothers or cousins we had seen march off to Fort Riley or Camp Funston would be marching back, all heroes.

WE HAD LICKED THE KAISER.

All of us joined in the victory.

There was some sadness, too. Not all the boys were coming back. One of my cousins, Elmer (Pete) Romick had been shot going over the top in France. We heard later that his rifle jammed and as he stopped momentarily to eject a stuck shell a German bullet struck him.

But the end of the war meant no more of our friends and relatives would suffer a similar fate. We were convinced peace was here forever and that democracy had been saved. It was a very real thing that night.

We boys and some of the men, too, had brought

shotguns. Suddenly there was a shout. Somebody carted a wooden barrel onto Main Street and it started to roll down the grade.

Spontaneously, the guns began to fire, the pellets impelling the barrel down the street at a speed that was incredible until the thing finally collapsed. That was fun.

Then Deacon Jones, the town marshal, shouldered his 12-gauge pump gun and called for the men to line up in front of the town pump.

"Shoulder arms," he ordered and six or eight men clicked their heels and straightened their shoulders, holding their shotguns in military fashion. The wives and youngsters cheered.

It sounds ridiculous now, but nothing could have been more in the spirit of the occasion at the time.

"One—two—three—four" Deacon, a tall, spare man, called off and the newly formed troop marched in the eerie darkness down Main street and back again. We boys trailed along shouting the one—two—three—fours in unison. An old grandfather carried a lantern. There were no electric lights in Maple Hill in 1918 and of course no radio to bring us more news.

Somebody got the idea of exploding an anvil. This was supposed to be the most gosh-awful way known to man to make a noise. My father was a little dubious about this as he had known that often an anvil was cracked and ruined with this trick.

But this was no night to protest. He opened the blacksmith shop and carried the heavy iron anvil out himself. Somebody ran to the hardware store for black powder.

The powder was packed into the hollow of the anvil, everybody warned to get back and a fuse was lighted.

There was a huge puff of fire, but no explosion.

"Load her up again," somebody called.

"Wait'll she cools down," a wiser head advised.

They waited until the anvil was only warm and packed the powder in again. Results were the same—big fire, no explosion.

Apparently exploding an anvil was a lost art in Maple Hill.

My father carried the anvil back into the shop and locked the door.

"Better get rid of this thing before somebody gets hurt," he explained.

By this time we had run out of anything to do. More lanterns were showing up here and there and people were gathering in little groups to talk. Even with nothing to do the excitement was such that we didn't want to go home.

But eventually the time had to come. Mothers and fathers said, "You kids better get home and get to bed because there'll be school tomorrow."

Tomorrow—what a wonderful day it and all others were going to be. That night we were completely convinced a better world lay ahead forever—we had won the war.

Dressing the Turkey

31

WHEN I read the latest government estimates on broiler and turkey production—more than three billion broilers and 130 million turkeys—I shuddered to think of how we would have managed to kill and dress our share of such numbers back in the old home town of Maple Hill when I was a boy.

We never talked about chickens in terms of millions, let alone billions, and turkeys were something special. Killing and dressing one chicken was a job and a turkey was a family project.

Nevertheless, we had chicken rather often, particularly during late summer, the season of fryers, and an occasional turkey on Thanksgiving.

The grocery stores in Maple Hill never sold a dressed chicken. Nobody even thought of such a thing; you had to kill and clean them yourself. Occasionally, you could buy live chickens which were kept in a coop over Fridays and Saturdays, but most of the time you raised the chickens or you bought them from neighbors or farmers.

We never used the word broiler, either. We had fried chickens. These were the young roosters that were the "surplus" in the raising of a flock of layers. Chickens were hatched only in the spring and by nature's way, they'd be about half roosters and the other half pullets. The pullets were kept for the laying flock in the fall; the roosters were eaten as fryers while they weighed about four to five pounds.

This meant we had frying chickens from July (when somebody had early chicks) to late August. After that we had roast or baked chicken—roosters and hens.

Our chickens got a balanced ration of whole corn and wheat we tossed out to them with the grasshoppers and other bugs that they found in the yard and fields. Some people still insist that those fryers tasted better than the modern broiler, but my own judgment is that memories are prejudiced by the voracious appetites of youth. They were good to eat then and they are good now.

Killing the chicken at our house was either a job for my mother, my brothers or me.

Frankly, our mother didn't like to kill chickens, but, out of necessity, she would. A sort of challenge to her was Mrs. Ida Carlson, a neighbor, who was widowed with three small children. Mrs. Carlson had no one to turn to, so when it came time to kill a chicken, she didn't hesitate. She'd grab the young rooster by the neck, give it a whirl, and off would come the head.

So, until we boys got big enough for the job, our

mother would wring the chicken's neck too. She said if Mrs. Carlson could do it, so could she. However, she always shut her eyes and turned her head.

When we boys became big enough to kill the chicken, we assumed that we could do anything a woman could do. But for some reason, a lack of strength or co-ordination, possibly, we couldn't wring the chicken's neck. So, we'd either put a broom stick over the neck and pull off the head, or chop it off with an ax. Since our aim with the ax wasn't always true, the broomstick method turned out to be the most accepted way.

The fried chicken dinner usually started out with specific directions from our mother.

"I've got the water heating in the teakettle," she'd say. "You boys catch the biggest fryer in the bunch and by the time you get it killed, the water will be boiling. Get along now."

If the chickens were in a pen, catching one was no problem, but if they were running loose, it could require quite a chase until we got the "big one" cornered.

Once the chicken was killed, we'd drop it into a big bucket and then pour the boiling water over it to loosen the feathers.

This job called for some discretion, because if the water were too hot and you kept the chicken in it too long, the skin would become cooked and would break. The trick was to get on just enough water to make picking of the feathers easy.

Most of the feathers did come off easily, but the pesky pin feathers took time to remove.

Once the feathers were off, we'd roll up a newspaper

and light it, and singe the bird in the flames to get rid of any tiny feathers missed. If it were a cold day, we'd take a lid off the kitchen range and drop some paper onto the fire to get a quick blaze for the singeing job.

Lawrence Romick, one of the Maple Hill farm boys I visited a lot, made a little more sport out of killing the chicken than we did in town. Lawrence shot them with a .22 rifle. The idea was to shoot them in the head and this took some marksmanship, when the young roosters were running loose in the barn yard.

Lawrence's mother not only picked off the feathers, but she skinned the chickens, too. She was the only person I ever knew who did this.

In these days of refrigeration, it is difficult to surmise how housewives would get along without this service. Obviously, before refrigeration, it was not possible to keep fresh meat long in the house before it was cooked. The farmyard chicken, however, was an available and quick source of meat for emergencies.

If, on a Sunday morning at church, our parents suddenly decided to invite the preacher and his wife for dinner, or some farm family who had driven into town, our mother would tell us boys to run home and catch another chicken, put a little more coal on the fire in the range and boil some water in the kettle. In almost no time at all, we could have the chicken ready for the frying pan.

Chickens also were a source of fresh meat for threshing crews—in fact, so often was chicken served that the crews, as they moved from one farm to the next, would welcome a change to roast beef. A roast beef dinner, of course, meant that the farm wife had to send somebody to town early in the morning to get the meat from the butcher shop. She wouldn't have had any way to keep it frozen for the day the threshers were at her farm. Chickens were always available.

Dressing a turkey was far more difficult than a frying chicken. In the first place, most of us had little experience. We never had turkeys except on Thanksgiving, and not every Thanksgiving. They simply were not that plentiful.

A check in old U. S. Department of Agriculture statistics shows why. As far back as 1930, farmers of this country were producing only about 16 million turkeys a year. This was when the country had a population of 120 million. Thus there was one turkey for each seven or eight persons. In recent years the per capita supply has been much greater.

In early days of this country, when the population was much smaller and more people lived on farms, the per capita supply of turkeys was larger than it was in the first part of the 20th century. By 1920, only one turkey was produced for each 15 persons. The industry has been growing ever since, largely because growers have been able to conquer disease problems.

For many years, farmers were giving up on turkeys because so many of them died before maturity. It used to be said that a turkey had only one ambition, and that was to die before man could kill him.

A disease called blackhead was the great killer and it would wipe out whole flocks. The disease seemed to be worse where farmers were trying to raise both turkeys and chickens. Most farmers gave up on the turkeys in favor of the chickens—until scientists developed better methods of raising the big birds.

Around Maple Hill, when I was a lad, only a few farmers tried to raise turkeys. The birds roosted in trees and had the run of the farm. If you wanted a turkey for Thanksgiving, you got your order in early.

Killing the turkey was a job too big for either our mother or us boys. We had to call on Dad. Our first attempt was almost a fiasco.

I held the big bird with its head lying on an old tree stump which was to serve as a chopping block. Dad was to wield the ax. His aim wasn't good, or perhaps I didn't hold the turkey in proper fashion. In any event, about all the ax hit was feathers. The turkey, only slightly wounded, broke loose from my grip and ran away. My brother, Bernard, and I gave chase and for a time it appeared our Thanksgiving dinner was going over the hill. But eventually we caught him, returned him to the chopping block and this time the aim of the ax was true.

We hung the turkey from the clothes line and began picking feathers. I can't recall, but I assume we had dipped it in boiling water. Most folks did, using a copper wash boiler, which was a standard part of the household equipment in those days.

Some people avoided such accidents as we had with the turkey by putting the big bird in a gunny sack, with its head sticking out a hole. By tying the sack, the bird was prevented from getting away.

I've heard people say that if they had to kill a chicken or turkey, they wouldn't eat them. I doubt this. If they were hungry and there was no other way to get the job done, they would go ahead.

Bounty on the Table

32

O N   T H E   day   before
Thanksgiving in the little school in my home town, we
always had a program in the afternoon. It was a
prelude to letting school out an hour or so early for the
Thanksgiving holidays.

The programs followed a traditional routine. Someone either read or told about the first Thanksgiving
and we paid our proper respects to those Pilgrims who
had come through their tortuous first year in this New
World and were thankful they had just enough to eat.
The point was made, and accepted, that we should be
very thankful for everything that we had in comparison to those early settlers. We gained an admiration
for them that as far as I am concerned remains to this
day and helps make every Thanksgiving meaningful.

After the Thanksgiving story, we sang songs, led by
our teacher, usually an "old maid" of about 20 (that
was how we boys spoke of her, even though secretly we

realized she was the prettiest young woman in town).

One of the songs invariably sung was the one about "over the river and through the wood, to grandfather's house we go."

The song went on to say:

The horse knows the way
To carry the sleigh
Through the wide and drifted snow.

Over the river and through the wood,
Oh, how the wind doth blow!
It stings the toes
And bites the nose
As over the ground we go.

And the final verse:
Over the river and through the wood—
Now grandmother's cap I spy!
Hurrah for the fun!
Is the pudding done?
Hurrah for the pumpkin pie!

The song always conjured up the picture, which hung in so many homes of those days, of a family in a sleigh just about to enter the gate to a farm home where grandpa and grandma stood on the porch waving them on.

I'm rather certain that no one in our school ever had traveled in a sleigh to grandpa's for Thanksgiving, but the song and picture contributed to the proper atmosphere for the holiday. The fact was, as far as I recall, when I was a boy there was just one old sleigh in town and it was considered an antique, although usable. A few farmers had sled runners for wagons which they used for feeding livestock and even for trips to town when the roads were covered by snow drifts.

After the singing was over, our teacher always asked that each pupil stand and tell why he personally was thankful this Thanksgiving season.

We boys invariably affirmed: We were thankful the next day was to be a holiday. We were thankful for the big dinner we were going to get.

The teacher just as invariably suggested that she had hoped for a little more originality, but she didn't complain or insist on a rerun because she was just as anxious as her pupils to conclude the program, dismiss school and head for home. For most of our teachers, home was in some other town.

At our home late that afternoon, we'd find our mother busy getting ready for the big dinner the next day and she'd have errands for us to run. These preparations for the dinner would be at least one way singularly in contrast to those of today. My mother would not have scanned the grocery ads to determine what she would buy and what was on sale for the holiday dinner.

There was a simple reason. There weren't any grocery ads and our little stores never had any sales. More than that, they seldom stocked anything extra for Thanksgiving. One exception, perhaps, was cranberries, which we bought in bulk and cooked before the holiday. The stores offered no dressed turkeys—in fact, no turkeys at all. If you wanted a turkey, you bought it from some farmer and you killed it yourself.

Turkeys were not always available around Maple

Hill, although we occasionally had them at our house. More often, we had a goose.

Goose or turkey, the bird had to be slaughtered the day before and this was one job turned over to my father, brother and me. Since we had this job only once or twice a year—at Christmas, as an example—we were not very adept. It sometimes was quite an ordeal, but we always got the job done—eventually.

For most of the food that would be bought today in a store, my mother had been making preparations all summer. By Thanksgiving time, our cellar was literally full with shelf after shelf of canned tomatoes, corn, beans, apples, peaches, cherries, elderberries, plums, chili sauce, catsup, mustard pickles, chow-chow, sweet pickles, dill pickles, beet pickles, watermelon pickles, strawberry jam, plum jelly, apple jelly and a dozen other delectable items. In fact, we could have had Thanksgiving dinner almost without going to the store at all.

There was one exception. Perhaps it was too much work or maybe she had had a bad experience, but my mother didn't like to can pumpkin. So we had to have "store bought" pumpkin for the Thanksgiving pie.

The baking had to be done the day before because the oven in our coal range would be busy Thanksgiving day for other things. Thus when we arrived home from school that Wednesday afternoon, we'd be greeted by one of the most appealing aromas on earth—that of home-baked bread.

My mother used a "starter" which she kept "alive" year in and year out in making bread. She made big loaves and a slice of her bread covered with farm-churned butter and topped with apple butter was a small meal by itself. In our family—and many others where the mothers baked the bread—we actually felt sorry for people who had to get along with the "store bought" kind. Homemade bread had the substance that would sustain a working man from one meal to the next. Wives with hard-working husbands felt a little guilty when they served baker's bread and there usually was "talk" about those women who did.

But one thing my mother knew was that she had to bake the bread ahead of time. A loaf of hot bread served to a hungry husband and sons disappeared discouragingly fast. In fact, it was a real treat when we were allowed to cut a loaf still hot from the oven.

That was one reason, of course, why the bread was baked the day before Thanksgiving.

The pumpkin pies were baked and allowed to cool overnight.

The day of the big dinner, the table would be loaded. At our house, in addition to the staples—the meat, bread, potatoes and other vegetables—we had a variety of pickles, jams and jellies from that cellar larder. It was a custom in nearly all country homes.

We'd eat until it seemed we could not get down another bite, always remembering, of course, that the pumpkin pie was yet to come. At the proper moment my mother would go to the kitchen, get a crock of cream and a hand beater. Then with strength and swiftness that always amazed me (as I as a boy never could duplicate it) she would flay the cream until it began to be a fluffy white mass. Then with a big spoon, she'd put a blob of whipped cream on each piece of pie.

But most important, she'd then put the crock of remaining cream on the table.

The way we boys worked it, the ingenious thing to do was to eat just enough of the pumpkin to get rid of the first blob of whipped cream. Then you asked for a second serving and you went through the process again. The old folks did it, too, and if anybody ever worried about putting on weight, they didn't mention it at the Thanksgiving table at our house.

With the dinner finally over, the women folk started cleaning up the dishes, a task that would take most of the afternoon. We'd always have some guests for dinner. We boys missed the after-dinner work.

My brother Bernard and I, John Carlson, who lived next door, and Brick Weaver, who lived across the way, would get our dogs and our single-barrel guns and head for the big bluestem-covered hills west of town. We felt that Thanksgiving day was made as much for hunting as for a big dinner. Others felt the same way and when you got into the country, you could hear the shotguns booming in the distance. Maybe that was in the tradition of the Pilgrims, too.

Despite the fact we had eaten until we were about to burst, before we left home Barnard and I would fill our pockets with homemade oatmeal cookies, just in case we got hungry on the hunt. We'd start eating them as soon as we began to follow the dogs across the fields.

Usually, on the big hill west of town, we'd scare up a jack-rabbit. The dogs would run him a quarter of a mile or so before they caught him or lost in the race. By this time we'd be on the other side of the hill and not far from Uncle Al Romick's farm, where Aunt

Nellie would be cleaning up the dishes after serving her big family and a group of relatives their Thanksgiving dinner. We'd stop to say hello and see if my cousin, Tom, wanted to join us in hunting, which, of course, he would. But before we'd leave, Aunt Nellie would invite us into the kitchen.

Just off this kitchen was one of those delightful little rooms that used to grace country homes—the pantry. And in this pantry on any fall or winter day, you'd always find an earthen jar containing Scotch scones, one of Aunt Nellie's specialties. Nobody made scones better than Aunt Nellie and it was no secret many of the Maple Hill women tried, even my mother.

Aunt Nellie always said the trick was a hot oven in a coal range. You had to build up the fire and create a big bed of hot coals. But other women could build up fires of hot coals, too. They insisted there must be some other secret. Apparently there wasn't. Her daughter, Mrs. Margaret McClelland, now makes scones just as good as her mother's.

Aunt Nellie gave out her recipe. Many Maple Hill homes still have it although Aunt Nellie has been gone many years. In fact we have it at our house in Kansas City and this is it:

1 pint sour cream.

¾ cup sugar.

1½ teaspoons soda.

1 teaspoon salt.

1½ cups raisins.

Stir vigorously, then add flour to make soft spongy dough. (Add flour one cup at a time, putting 1 teaspoon of baking powder into each cup.) Use a sharp sour—but not strong—bitter cream.

The amount of flour used depends upon the thickness of the cream. Place dough on floured board and knead until the right consistency. Roll until quite thin. Cut and bake in a very hot oven.

That's just the way Aunt Nellie said it ought to be done and she brought the recipe with her from Scotland.

Aunt Nellie would give each of us boys a couple of the scones and we'd be on our way. Late in the afternoon we'd come back across Uncle Al's farm, over the big hill again and wearily trek into town. The coal-oil lamp would be lighted and sitting on the library table in the front room at home. My mother would say we'd better bring in another bucket of coal as she heated water in the kettle for tea. On the dining room table under a cloth cover (we had no refrigerator) there'd be the leftovers from dinner—some cold meat, a few pieces of pumpkin pie and even a little whipped cream in the crock, a cake that hadn't been cut at noon, plenty of jams, jellies and pickles for which we'd now have room and, of course, the home-baked bread.

If there's anything better than a Thanksgiving day dinner, it is the supper from the leftovers after a boy has spent an afternoon traipsing with his dogs over Kansas hills. What a way to end the day!

And we'd been right the day before at school:

We were thankful for the holiday.

We were thankful for the big dinner.

The Pilgrims should have had it half so good.

Country Store
At Christmas Time

33

For pure delight in memories of Christmas time nothing is brighter for me than the recollections of the two "general merchandise" stores that served Maple Hill, when I was a boy.

And yet, when I try today to rationalize the enthusiasm I once had for these stores in the holiday season I find it extremely difficult because they actually had so little to display that I wonder where I got the thrill. But I did and so did a lot of other boys and girls, and perhaps our parents, too.

Our two stores were one-story affairs. Dave Stewart's store was in a two-story stone building, but the top floor was used by the Masonic and Woodman lodges. R. T. Updegraff's place was a one-story frame building. Both had warehouses at the back where sacks, boxes and barrels of merchandise were kept.

The stores were divided within about the same. Along one side were the grocery and meat counters.

222

Down through the center were tables for such items as overalls, jackets, hats, caps, overshoes and the like. On the other side yard goods were displayed at a long counter where there were stools on which women could sit as they examined the bolts of cloth.

Near the front was the candy counter a glass case which held trays of lemon drops, gum drops, licorice pipes, jaw-breakers, candy corn, and peppermints.

There were a lot of other things in the stores, too, of course, such as sacks of potatoes, onions and apples. When you asked for a gallon of coal oil, a clerk took the empty can back to the warehouse to fill it from a barrel. He did the same for vinegar.

In fact, the stores ordinarily were utilitarian to the nth degree as there was no effort whatever to dress up any product. They had things to sell, and people knew that was where they were going to buy them.

But at Christmas time everything was different—at least for a small youngster. The overalls, overshoes, coats and jackets were removed from the center counters and in their stead came new toys plus all the old ones that hadn't sold the year before and had been stored in boxes in the warehouse.

There were no electric lights to gleam, no moving Santa Clauses or dolls, no miniature trains ducking in and out of tunnels—just sleds, dolls, wind-up gadgets, balls, punching bags, popguns—there must have been more because the counters seemed so full.

You walked round and round, touching this one and admiring that one, as your folks shopped for the groceries. If something was gone one day you wondered who would be the lucky youngster—maybe you?

Mom and Dad would talk slyly to Mr. Stewart or Mr. Updegraff. Dad would say, "Dave, do you think Santa Claus might have a sled just like that one on the counter, if we'd put in an order?"

Mr. Stewart would turn to us boys and ask if we'd like for him to put in a good word to Santa about that sled.

"Aw, we know there ain't no Santa Claus, you can't fool us," we'd reply.

"Well, you'd like that sled, wouldn't you?" Mr. Stewart would continue.

"Yep," we'd say hopefully, looking Dad right in the eye.

Christmas morning we'd be properly surprised. There was a brand new sled.

The candy counter changed, too, at Christmas time. Trays were piled high with colored candies, mostly red. Instead of buying a penny's worth, which was our usual purchase, with delight we'd hear Dad say to Mr. Updegraff, "R. T., put me up about 50 cents of that Christmas mixture."

Mr. Updegraff would take one hand scoop load and then another to the scales on the counter. The candy from the scoop would dribble onto the scales until they balanced at the proper mark. Then he'd reach into the glass case again, get another handful and toss it onto the pile.

"Merry Christmas from me, too," he'd say as he poured the candy into a regular grocery sack.

Gee whiz, a big sack of candy. Christmas was great!

Along about Christmas eve the counter in the center

of the store was getting empty. Things looked kind of skimpy in a way, but this was a good sign, too. We weren't so dumb.

Anything not sold went back to the warehouse. We didn't have after-Christmas sales.

Christmas time or any other time, the store was a great place to visit, especially on Saturday night. Everybody came into town on Saturday night to buy groceries and "settle up." We didn't have time payment plans such as today, but practically everybody "charged it" until Saturday night.

My brothers and I trailed along with our father when he went to settle up. We had a special reason.

It would be on Saturday night and Mom long since would have been in first one store and then the other to sit on the stools at the dry goods counters to visit with the farm women in town for the evening. We boys would be chasing up and down the sidewalks with no real purpose in mind.

Dad would have gone to the barber shop for his shave and he would have visited with the men up and down the street. Occasionally he'd cross over to our blacksmith shop, and light the lamp at the dusty desk where he kept his books, so that some farmer could settle up with him.

Mostly they'd say, "Just fill out the check, John, I'll sign it." Farmer's hands usually weren't in good condition for writing. But their signatures were good at the Stockgrowers State bank.

Actually, not too much cash changed hands even on Saturday night. Farmers either paid by check or, at the stores, traded in their eggs, butter and chickens for

225

groceries. A farm wife who brought in enough eggs to pay for the groceries and still had a little left over was looked upon as a smart woman. People would say, "There are folks who will get ahead."

Eventually all this trading would be over. Farmers would load their families into wagons or their Model T's and head out the dark roads for home. There'd be no more boys to run up and down the streets. Only a few people would be in the stores. Dad then would go into Stewart's and remark casually, "What's it amount to tonight, Dave?"

Mr. Stewart would add quickly the purchases Mom had made that evening. There would be little slips for purchases made each day of the week. While Dad was writing out the check, the grocer would fill a small sack with candy. Grocer Updegraff would do the same thing—we divided our trade.

Personal service played a major role in the small town grocery store. Both grocers, for instance, had delivery wagons. Updegraff had a pretty, all-black mare that pulled his wagon, while Stewart used a large dapple gray. It was customary for the folks in town to call in their orders each day, particularly for meats, as few had ice boxes. The most usual order from our house was "A quarter's worth of steak." I don't recall the weight, but that apparently was the right amount for a meal. Working in a blacksmith shop, my father needed good food. We bought lots of "boiling beef" and soup was a frequent dish on our table, particularly in cold weather. In fact, vegetable soup was kept warm from one meal to the next on the back lid of the coal range. Nobody ever made better soup than that.

226

At the store, meat was kept in a cooler cooled with cakes of ice in warm weather. When you placed your order, the grocer lifted a huge piece of beef from the cooler to the meat block and cut the piece you wanted. His cleaver hung on a hook on the block, while his saw hung on a hook overhead.

Butter, too, was kept in the cooler. If you were particular, you checked with the grocer to see if Mrs. So and So had brought her butter to town. While there were some things people didn't talk about, it was no secret that some farm women made better butter than others. A few molded their butter with pretty designs and the mold became their trademark.

The grocer ladled lard out of a wood tub and put it into little wood trays. Lard must have been expensive because I can recall the women discussing recipes and they'd say something was good, but "it just takes too much lard."

Glamour played no part in the old store, and the built-in maid service they talk about so much today in reference to oven-ready products just hadn't been discovered. A chicken, for instance, was purchased alive. The grocer went to a coop at the back of the store, caught a young rooster, tied its feet together and you took it home to kill it yourself.

No doubt the housewife today is much happier with the modern store. No doubt, too, the youngsters today would think the Christmas counters of the old stores were pretty drab affairs. I guess I would, too, now—but thrills came easier once upon a time.

Electricity
Changed Rural Life

34

I CAN'T recollect for certain, but I believe my mother put up the first outdoor Christmas lights in our old home town. This was in 1929.

One reason I can't be sure is that I already had been in Kansas City several years at that time. We didn't have electricity in Maple Hill when I was a boy. The power lines were extended from Rossville to Maple Hill in 1924. Power came from the Kansas Power and Light Company in Topeka.

My folks had remodeled our old home in 1929 and were quite proud of the results. So, as part of the celebration, my mother bought some strings of outdoor lights and decorated the part of the house that faced the main traveled street. When I visited them that Christmas I thought the bright lights were wonderful and so did other people from around the countryside who drove by at night just to see the sight.

There could have been others in Maple Hill at the time, but those on our home were the first that I had seen.

My point is that it hadn't been customary for many people to decorate their homes with Christmas lights in rural Kansas towns. Also rural people first experiencing the pleasures of electricity were inclined to seek ways to conserve on its use rather than expand it. It took a while to get used to a regular monthly bill.

None of the farms around Maple Hill was decorated with electric Christmas lights for the simple reason that they weren't served with electric power. Some of them got it in the mid-1930s when the rural electrification program was inaugurated. But the great bulk of the farms was not reached with the power lines until after World War II.

Drive any direction from Kansas City mid-December across rural Kansas or Missouri and you will see farm homes, some of them far off the main highways, gaily decorated with Christmas lights, a most cheery sight in the darkness of a winter night in the country.

But this is a development far more recent than most of us in cities realize. Prior to REA electricity was almost a rarity on farms. This was recalled in a book, "Rural Electric Facts," published by the National Rural Electric Co-operative Association and edited by Donald H. Cooper. The book was designed to be a source of reference material on what it refers to as "an American success story."

I can't recall what spurred the power companies to begin extending their lines from major cities such as

Topeka to little communities such as Maple Hill in the 1920s, but it certainly was a welcome move. When we had our old home wired, we did just like all the other folks in town and had a drop light put in the center of the ceiling in each room, an extra socket put in the kitchen for an iron and another in the front room by the library table for a reading lamp.

I wasn't living there, but I was home often enough to know what they were doing. People were thinking almost 100 per cent about LIGHT and had little thought of all the other dozens of services now performed by electricity.

When the folks remodeled the home, they had had a few years of experience with electricity and therefore had new outlets put in each room.

We always celebrated every holiday at our house and this, of course, included Christmas. We'd have some sort of a tree, usually a branch cut from a cedar on a farm nearby. Prior to electricity, we had decorated with strings of cranberries and popcorn and other things my mother contrived. She was good at "making do" with what was available and she always was willing to try anything new, which may explain why she was the first or among the first to put up the outdoor Christmas lights.

However, we never lighted our tree with candles as some did. Even though they'd put a bucket of water beside the tree just in case of fire, we thought the danger was too great. Maple Hill, as most rural communities, had had bad experiences with fire and we knew that in most instances when flames got a start the house and everything in it were destroyed.

One of the first improvements at our home, electrically, was accomplished by my youngest brother, Don, who still was a youngster when the power lines reached Maple Hill.

On the back side of our big yard stood a garage, a coal shed, tool shed and the outdoor toilet. When the electricians wired the house, they also put a light in the garage. Don bored holes through the wall of the garage, then the coal house, tool house and outdoor toilet, ran insulated wires through the holes and installed a light in the toilet.

Laughing about this later, Don recalled that when you turned on the light you had to shut the door. But on the other hand, you could see to read the catalogues.

He always tried to figure out some way to provide instant heat but never was able to come up with anything feasible.

When the old home was remodeled, a bathroom and inside toilet were installed. The glory of the light in the outdoor one was short-lived.

Prior to REA, about the only farms that had electricity were those on the borders of towns in the heavily-populated states such as New York, Pennsylvania and California. Some had their own individual plants. In 1934, 10.9 per cent of all the farms in the United States were served by electricity. But in Kansas only 7.6 per cent of the farms had electric current and the percentage in Missouri at 6.4 was even smaller. Oklahoma and Texas had electricity for less than 3 per cent of their farms.

Curiously, as more little towns got power lines and

reaching out to farms came into the realm of possibility, two forces acted against the development. On the one side were the power companies who insisted they couldn't afford to install lines for rural services. In effect, they pooh-poohed the idea that farmers wanted or needed electricity or that they could use enough to pay for it if they got it.

On the other side were farmers who had been getting along with coal oil lights for generations and didn't see why they shouldn't continue. Here again, they were thinking only of lights. Electricity was regarded as a luxury, not a service.

Eventually both sides were proved wrong. It was possible to serve farms with electric lines and when they got the electricity, farmers turned the power into the cheapest source of labor they ever had had.

Obviously light still is important on farms, but the other uses of electricity far surpass it in total wattage.

There's a story they used to tell that illustrated how the farmers first regarded electricity and that monthly bill when the rural lines first became a reality. Remember, these were depression years.

Two farm widows lived alone in houses not far apart. They visited often. One was commenting one day on how she had a light in her bedroom and a light and an iron in the kitchen, but she just couldn't use enough electricity to cover the $3.50 minimum called for in her bill each month. It worried her that she was paying for electricity that she could not use.

"I've solved that problem," the other widow commented. "Just as I go to bed I take the bulb out of the socket and let the electricity run out on the floor all night long."

This may be a little exaggerated, but it still is a good indication of what strangers rural people were to electricity when it first became available to them.

A man who long had been interested in rural power development was President Franklin D. Roosevelt. It is rather ironic, however, that his first major step toward rural lines was part of a general program to relieve unemployment rather than to get electric power to farms. May 11, 1935, he signed an executive order establishing the Rural Electrification Administration. The authorization for this was the Emergency Relief Appropriation Act of early 1935. Thus the goal was to give more people work in putting up rural power lines, but not much was accomplished because few of the rural unemployed knew anything about electrical installations.

The next year the Rural Electrification Act was passed which created the rural co-ops and started the ball rolling. Under the act farmers could band together in a co-operative to build their own lines, for which, in most cases, they could get power from the nearest city plant. To finance the project, the co-op could borrow money from the government first at 3 and later at 2 per cent interest. But the act also provided that the power companies also could borrow money from the government to extend lines out to farmers. A few did, but most wouldn't. They were insisting that it would cost $2,000 or better a mile and that farmers wouldn't use enough current to pay for the investment.

One of the companies that did venture in the program was Arkansas Power and Light. It began putting in rural ines in 1938. I drove down to Harrison, Ark., to get a story on one of the first installations. At the light company office in Harrison I suggested it would add a little drama if we could visit a farm with a log house. I thought electricity in a log cabin would indicate quite a bridge between the old and the modern eras.

"That will be easy," one of the officials told me. He rode with me out to a farm where a log home had been electrified. However, it was a rather comfortable log house, not a pioneer's cabin. It had a wide porch.

The middle-aged farm couple were ecstatic about the new service. And they had a brand new radio. This, almost inevitably, was the first appliance purchased once the lights had been turned on in a rural home. Next came the iron, washing machine, toaster and a myriad of other household appliances. The big motors that were to operate feed machinery and do other major chores on the farm came later.

The Arkansas company was hiring local farmers and using poles cut in the area for putting up the new lines. They were doing this at around $800 a mile and giving much-needed wages to the farmers. In fact, all over the country, the new co-ops in the late 1930s were finding out that they could put up the power lines at between $700 and $900 a mile. If a power company wanted to put up a line it had to buy easement rights across a farm. When farmers went together in a co-op, they didn't see any sense in charging themselves for such easements. There were other differences, too, but the co-ops proved the job could be done at far less than the power companies had contended—on borrowed, low interest government money, of course, but the rate of repayment has been almost perfect. Only two small rural electric co-ops have been foreclosed on by the government since the program started in 1936.

The rural electrification program was just getting well under way when World War II brought it to an abrupt halt because of shortages of copper and other supplies. Meanwhile those farmers who had been fortunate enough to get electric power had learned how to use it to advantage.

Electricity was the greatest labor-saver that ever came to farms.

Despite all the talk about the good old days, I never have heard anyone from a farm or rural community express a yearning for the time before electricity. You had to live without it to realize what a wonderful thing it was to switch, in the matter of an instant, from the days of the coal oil lamp to LIGHT. The gay holiday lights on farm homes across the countryside celebrate two occasions, Christmas and the modern era.

The Gift Lamp

35

I've always been happy over the fact that I was a boy in Maple Hill during a period when there was no problem in our family or in most others in our little town on what to get each other for Christmas.

There were so many things we wanted and could use that the only difficulty was in getting the money to buy them. The result was that every member of the family fully appreciated anything he found under the Christmas tree.

To be real honest, we didn't always have a Christmas tree, because evergreens were not very plentiful around Maple Hill and nobody at that time ever heard of trees being shipped in. Occasionally, we were able to get a large limb from a big cedar on a nearby farm and my mother made that do. Since we had no electricity then, we didn't have lights for a tree and what decorations we had were homemade.

236

Nor did we have a fireplace with a mantel on which to hang our stockings. But we did hang our stockings on something in the front room—the only room with a stove other than the kitchen—and our presents were piled underneath them. The stockings, our regular long black ones were filled with candy and oranges.

On a cold Christmas morning, the very first action was to open the draft on the Round Oak stove to start the fire roaring. Then my brothers and I, still in the long underwear in which we had slept, started to open packages.

I must choose my words carefully here for I might give two wrong impressions. One would be that we lived in poverty and that wasn't the case at all. We were abundantly supplied with all the necessities—lots of good food, ample shelter and sufficient clothing.

Nor would I want to suggest that in today's affluent society, there are not millions of families who are needy.

On the other hand, so many more things are available today even to relatively poor people, and certainly to people with modest or better means, that any comparison with Maple Hill of 50 to 60 years ago would put us old home towners in a pretty bad light.

One thing for certain, when we were youngsters in Maple Hill, we never had a football game where every boy brought his own football, or a baseball game where every player had a glove. In fact, even in high school, our team had just one football. It was "the ball" we took when we played Alma, Eskridge or Rossville. And the schools in those towns also supplied one ball.

But come to think of it, you need only one ball.

It so happened that the Maple Hill of my day existed at a time when little towns of Kansas were just on the verge of going modern. Motor cars were coming into general use. A few main highways were being graveled. Electricity was not far down the line.

It was a time when more and more things that everybody wanted were becoming available. Most of them are necessities now, but in our home, they were luxuries. That's why we appreciated them so much.

In fact, these reminiscenses were sparked by the salvaging of an old electric lamp from our home at Maple Hill.

After the death of our stepmother, our home stood empty briefly for the first time in almost 70 years. My brother, Don Turnbull of Kansas City, went through the old house and brought the lamp home to me, because he remembered how proud my mother and father were of it.

Electricity came to Maple Hill in the early 1920s. We did what all the other families in town did in getting our houses wired. We had a drop light with a white shade put in the center of each room and one floor socket put in each room. It seemed ample at the time.

An electric light in every room (and one even in the outdoor toilet) was such improvement over anything we had had before that we weren't thinking about all the extra conveniences that some day might come.

We had been living with coal oil lamps on which the glass chimneys had to be cleaned each day. And we also had a Coleman gasoline table lamp, which, except for the nuisance of keeping up the air pressure, provided excellent illumination.

We also had a Coleman lantern for my father's blacksmith shop. It had replaced a huge brass coal oil lamp with a big brass shade that hung on an iron rod from the ceiling. Somebody got that lamp as an antique. Our family wasn't antique-minded, and we failed to save any such things.

The Coleman lantern was replaced at the blacksmith shop by an electric light bulb hanging from its wire directly over the anvil.

Electricity came to our home town just after I had gone to Kansas City to be a reporter on *The Star*. The very first Christmas after the old home was wired, I bought my folks a brass table lamp with a shade made of sections of stained glass at a chandelier store.

My parents set the lamp on the library table in the front room. They thought it was about the prettiest thing they'd ever had. And it was pretty. Neighbors came in to admire it. The whole family could sit around the table and read from the light it spread from its two bulbs.

Down through the years, the lamp was guarded carefully, even after a new chandelier had been installed and floor lamps acquired. Once it was knocked over and the brass stem broken. My father got a piece of brass rod from the blacksmith shop and repaired it good as new.

"Be careful around that lamp," my stepmother would admonish the grandchildren. "John (my father) is so proud of that he won't stand for any foolishness."

The children were careful and I guess that is why the glass shade is still unbroken today.

That's the kind of appreciation that seemed to prevail at our house.

I recall the Christmas my father gave our mother a new kitchen cabinet.

The kitchen cabinet replaced an old cupboard. The cupboard was just a set of shelves with doors. But the new cabinet was an ingenious device. It had a bin for flour and a smaller bin for sugar. All you had to do was put a bowl under the flour bin, pull on a little slide and the flour would flow into the bowl. A similar action got sugar from the sugar bin. There were little shelves on the upper doors for spice cans. The main upper shelves were for dishes. Down below were the pots and pans.

The new cabinet was placed in a corner only a step or two from the big coal range. It was a labor-saver for my mother and we were really proud of it. Even the neighbor kids were invited in to see it. Of course, whenever anybody in our neighborhood got anything new all of us shared in the pleasure.

The advent of electricity enabled families in Maple Hill to catch up with city friends on all kinds of gadgets—electric toasters, mixers and, when they became available, radios.

We'd had a device for toasting bread even when I was at home. It was a wire frame affair with two handles. You put the slice of bread between two layers of wire and then held it closely over the hot lids on the stove. We didn't use it often because it was too much trouble. Also, homemade bread didn't toast very well anyway. The slices were too thick for one thing.

The first radio in our home at Maple Hill was another Kansas City purchase. It was a four-tube affair, with three sets of ear phones. My father always insisted they got more pleasure out of it than any radio they ever had, although later they had modern models and eventually television. But there's a special thrill in getting something for the first time.

For a period of several years, the one present my brother Bernard and I wanted was shotgun shells. Hunting was our principal winter diversion. We skated when Mill Creek was frozen and went sledding when the big hill west of town was covered with snow, but we could hunt at any time from late fall through January.

We could buy six black powder, 12-gauge shotgun shells for a quarter at the hardware store. If we killed a rabbit or a squirrel, we could dress him and sell the meat to someone in town for 20 to 25 cents. This meant money to buy some more shells, unless we bought something else. Which, naturally, we often did. Thus we were almost always short of funds when it came to buying the ammunition. And we didn't like to run to our father for such money. He always was rather generous, but operated under the theory that if you were big enough to hunt with shotgun, you should earn the money for the shells. Often we'd go hunting with only three or four shells in our pockets for our single-barrel guns.

But on Christmas, we were overwhelmed because we'd find two full boxes each, a total of 50 shells. Fifty shells and two weeks of vacation was about as near heaven as we hoped to get at that time. We hardly could wait for Christmas dinner to be over so we could load our pockets with maybe 10 or 12 shells and head for the creeks and the hills.

Nothing that our parents gave us thrilled us more than the two whole boxes of shells—which cost at that time, 90 cents a box. I wonder if they appreciated how easy we made their Christmas shopping chore.

We always had all the candy we needed—but never as much as we wanted. We had cousins living in another city in Kansas who owned a candy store. On Christmas, they would send us a box of the traditional holiday hard varieties and this was wonderful for two reasons. First, a box of several pounds of hard candy is a lot of candy, and second, the box came in the mail.

There was nothing that added more glamour to a Christmas present than to have it come in the mail. You went to the post office and as you emptied your box of the routine letters and the daily paper, the post mistress would calmly announce that she had a package for you. At Christmas, you knew it had to be something good.

I still like "cheap" candy maybe because of the memories of those Christmas days.

As I recall, there were just two bicycles in our town when Bernard and I were youngsters. We'd spend hours looking at the pictures of bikes in the mail order catalogues, but we didn't expect to get one because our folks explained they couldn't afford it. Actually, so few boys had bikes, we didn't expect one.

But when Bernard finished high school and joined me in Kansas City on the staff of *The Star,* the first Christmas after his arrival, he and I pooled funds with our father to get a bicycle for Don, who at 11 years of age was still at home. And I don't know who got the biggest pleasure from it—Don or Bernard, my father and I who had managed to buy the first bicycle for anyone in the Turnbull family. It was, so to speak, a milestone. Don still says that was the biggest Christmas of his life.

However, by that time, half a dozen or more boys in Maple Hill had bicycles. In other words, it had become a common thing. It was a sign of the changing times. An era was ending.

Mothers Made
The Sunday School

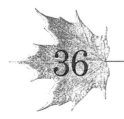

36

In writing about the old home town, I already have reminisced on Christmas eve in the little church at Maple Hill some years ago, but I have not paid full tribute to the mothers who made nearly all our church activities possible.

In our little town, particularly as far as children were concerned, the mothers and the functions which had church sponsorship were virtually synonymous. The regular Sunday school was a good example.

It was the mothers—(who must have been pretty young because this was 40 to 50 years ago and some are still alive) who planned and put on the Christmas pageant. In a town of our size there was no public library, nor any other source of material for Christmas entertainment. It was up to the ingenuity of the mothers involved to come up with their own inventions.

This included costumes. The two small general

merchandise stores, which supplied both groceries and "dry goods," had only the raw materials for costumes.

There was little or no real poverty in the community, at least in my boyhood memories. While there were people of affluence, few that I recall had college educations and many of the mothers, including my own, had not had four full years of high school. It is only in recollection that these facts become apparent because they were considered of no import at the time.

If any of the mothers had any special religious training, other than attendance at Sunday school and church, I never knew about it. Yet they did their best to teach. The Christmas story was one both teachers and youngsters could understand.

Our Sunday school had its quarterlies which came from a religious supply house. From these we got the reading material for our lessons.

The church had one large room, the sanctuary, and one back room which ran across the width of the building. Sunday school opened with the singing of hymns while one of the mothers played the organ or piano. Two or three women in town had had music lessons and could play well. Others, such as my mother, played by ear. They took their turns. The preacher or the Sunday school superintendent stood up in front to lead the singing. That was part of his job.

With the hymn singing over, we divided into classes, two groups going to the back room and the others assembling in the various corners of the sanctuary.

Obviously, there was always some confusion.

Our teachers were our mothers, with few exceptions. Occasionally an older high school girl would take a class, or perhaps even a schoolteacher. Our school boards tried to hire teachers who could sing, play the piano and teach a Sunday school class. Such talents were extremely advantageous and important in a rural community. People didn't like it if a teacher went to her own home in some other town every weekend.

One of my teachers was Lillian Oliver, a high school girl, who in an effort to keep order acted like a schoolteacher—she slapped me smartly because I had hit Brick Weaver on the side of the head. I went home after Sunday school furious and determined never to return. But it didn't work. My mother had me back the next Sunday. What made me so mad was that Miss Oliver hadn't even asked what Brick had done. He really had let me have it with a pin.

But it wouldn't have made much difference. The mothers and the teachers stuck together. In fact, there was an understanding among the mothers that wherever the youngsters were playing, the mother on hand was "boss." For instance, when I went to play in Weavers' yard, I was admonished, "You do exactly as Mrs. Weaver says." I guess it was one way of mothers sharing the load.

After the lesson in Sunday school, the congregation reassembled. The collection was taken and posted on a board in front of the room, where it could be compared with the totals of the previous week. Usually it would read something like this:

246

Attendance	Collection
Today	$2.71
43	

Attendance	Collection
Last Sunday	$1.92
39	

It should be obvious that most of our contributions were nickels and pennies.

A final hymn closed Sunday school and the youngsters rushed out. Mostly only the older ones had to stay for church.

Our little town comprised its own school district. In the rural areas around were several one-room schools. Children from these schools attended Sunday school, and often this was the principal way we got acquainted with the "country kids." It is difficult to believe now, but there was a distinction then, particularly among the girls.

Some of the "town" mothers had to admonish their daughters to be nice to the girls from the farm and make them welcome. Often the farm girls were so bashful this was difficult. A little later, when schools were consolidated, all this distinction vanished—a good thing.

Christian Endeavor was the gathering place for the teenagers, Sunday evening. A young woman schoolteacher was almost a necessity for keeping this organization going, the mothers being less appreciated as leaders than when the children were smaller.

Our church had a special lighting system using gasoline as a fuel. It had an air pressure tank which had to be pumped up before (and during) each service with a motor car tire pump. This, of course, was the first chore before Christian Endeavor could come to order. There always were boys on hand for the job.

Mothers of the church helped plan the parties and picnics. The picnics were in Steele Romick's grove on Mill Creek. Picnics, like Christmas, helped build Sunday school attendance.

The picnics began at the church—that is, everybody gathered there with baskets. Mr. Romick or sometimes one of the older McClelland boys would supply a hayrack with a gentle team. It would be a jolty ride, but lots of fun. We youngsters all together would make a loud ah-ah-ah-ah sound and the jolting of the wagon would give it a thrilling vibration.

We'd stop at the depot to pick up a freezer of ice cream, shipped out from Topeka on the local freight.

The mothers provided games for the afternoon, served the food and saw to it that nobody was severely injured. When the ice cream, the chicken, the pie, cake and pickles were all gone, the picnic would be over; then we'd have the hayrack ride back to the church.

Next Sunday the figures on the Sunday school blackboard would read, "Attendance 52, collection $5.12."

In our family, we had to go to Sunday school in the morning if we wanted to play baseball in the afternoon. This was mother's ruling. My father, who had been born in Scotland, had not been allowed even to whistle on Sunday. Somehow the severity hadn't paid off; at least he made no effort to enforce the rule in this country. He wouldn't work in the blacksmith shop on

Sunday, but he didn't have time to take off for Sunday school picnics during the week. This was a mother's job.

Our church had a belfry with a trap door. If you could get through the door, you could find your way on rafters to the ceiling over the sanctuary. This was a rather dangerous adventure because it was obvious if you slipped from a rafter you would break through the ceiling.

In the quiet between Sunday school and church one Sunday morning Brick Weaver, Tom Romick and I managed to climb from a stepladder, to a window ledge and then on through the trap door. We went from the belfry to the space over the ceiling and under the roof where we thought it would be fun to listen to the church service. We knew, however, that we would have to get down before the service was over or we would be in serious trouble.

Then we discovered we couldn't get down. While we had been able to reach the window ledge from the ladder going up, we couldn't get a toe-hold coming down. We got scared and evidently created a disturbance, because someone came out to see what was going on.

Church service let out early that day. Mrs. Weaver, whose home was nearby, called Brick's grandfather who had been picking cherries. He came to our rescue with a ladder.

This incident gave me special appreciation of a story told when a chautauqua was held in our church some years later; the church, of course, had to serve for any event that called for an auditorium.

A quartet of young soldiers in uniform, just back from World War I, gave a program interspersed with humorous stories. They told a joke about some high school girls climbing into a church attic. One slipped and her leg broke through the ceiling, where it was visible to the congregation attending services below. The minister quickly proclaimed:

"Verily, I say that if any man looks up at that ceiling, he shall be stricken blind."

One man in the congregation immediately slapped a hand over one eye and, looking up, remarked:

"Well, here's where I risk one eye."

I've heard the joke many times since, and always I have known that somebody could have fallen through the ceiling in the church at Maple Hill, although I never heard of any girls climbing into the attic.

Rivaling the chautauqua story as a vivid recollection was the illustration used by a minister at a revival meeting to press the point that religion isn't something to be used in times of trouble only.

He told about a farmer who, putting on shingles high on the roof of his barn, started to slip down. "Save me Lord," he screamed, "Save me. Save me!"

Then suddenly with a great such of relief he proclaimed:

"Never mind, Lord. I'm caught on a nail."

Revivals were the source of a controversy in our town. My mother belonged to a group which thought the church needed a little stimulation each year, particularly to bring in new members. Others were of the opinion revivals lacked dignity or sanctity. For a time we compromised and had rather dignified revival meetings. They brought some fine song leaders to town.

The church is still active at Maple Hill—bigger than ever before, which is contrary to the experience in many rural areas. It has been remodeled; a community hall has been added and even a parking lot. The church has an electric organ and a choir the equal of many of those in small churches in Kansas City. One young man trained in the choir became a member of Kansas State University's glee club as a freshman student.

On rare occasions I have attended Maple Hill church functions in recent years, and I notice paper money in the collection plate, not just pennies and nickles. The young people are less bashful and perhaps more willing to participate in the church functions.

Only one thing appears about the same—it is the mothers who are keeping things going.

Hard Work for Mothers

37

FAR be it from me to enter into the controversy over women's lib. I'm perfectly willing to leave that to those who seem to be most interested in it. However, it did occur to me a few mornings ago that without any political movement women have gained many advantages in certain ways since my mother was rearing three boys.

It was the morning recently when the temperature hit zero and it just happened that my wife had some washing to do. She put the clothes in an automatic washer, dried them in a dryer and all this was done in a warm basement. The fact it was zero outside mattered not at all.

This couldn't have happened when we boys were youngsters at Maple Hill. In the first place, our mother had neither an electric washer nor a dryer. And she couldn't use the hand-powered washer we owned because it sat on the back porch. This "torture"

252

machine was all right in summer weather, but was useless when it was freezing.

A few people had "washhouses," little frame buildings that sat in the yard near the back door, where there was a flat-topped stove for heating water and a place for the hand-powered washing machine. But even the washhouse was not a comfortable place in zero weather.

So our mother did the same as all other housewives in Maple Hill and the surrounding farm country on winter washdays. She used a copper boiler, and a couple of galvanized tubs on a wood bench in the kitchen. The clothes were rubbed on a wash board in soapy water in one tub and then dropped into a tub of rinse water. The rinse water was given a healthy supply of bluing—to make the clothes white.

First step on washday was to heat the water in the copper boiler, which called for a hot fire in the kitchen stove. I helped pump the water and got the coal for the stove, but I didn't do any of the washing. As I recall, the white clothes were boiled in the copper boiler before being rubbed on the washboard. However, since I wasn't a direct participant, my recollections on the exact process are hazy.

I do recall that the clothes were taken out of the boiling water with a stick and transferred to the tub for rubbing. The clothes stick was a household fixture and something we boys didn't take away.

The real cold part of the washing came after the clothes had been taken from the rinse water and had to be hung up to dry. We had a cellar that served for storing canned fruit, potatoes and apples, but it was no place to hang clothes. In fact, not a home in Maple Hill had a warm basement; only one or two had furnaces; all the others were just like ours, they had a big stove in the front room and the range in the kitchen.

My mother would string a line across the kitchen and hang a few clothes on it. A few more would be draped over chairs. But the bulk of the washing, particularly the long underwear and overalls, had to be hung on the line outdoors.

The long underwear would freeze, and apparently "froze dry." Late in the afternoon, we boys would help gather it in and it would be like picking skeletons off the line. The drying process would be completed in the house. It is easy to understand now why we had only one change of underwear a week—every Saturday night.

I would hasten to explain that we did not look upon our way of life at Maple Hill as one of hardships. We regarded ourselves as modern and felt sorry for the pioneers. We had most of the available conveniences of the day in our house and more than would be found in some of the poorer homes. For one thing, we had a good well with a pump just outside the kitchen door for bringing water and a pump in the kitchen that brought soft water from the cistern. Only a small percentage of the country homes boasted both these conveniences.

It is difficult to exaggerate the importance of plentiful water supplies in a home. Of course, we couldn't turn on faucets and get either hot or cold water. But at our home we did have an ample supply from the well and the cistern. We had a "reservoir" on the kitchen range that held about five gallons and when the fire was going, this water would be kept relatively hot. You would dip out enough for the wash basin in the kitchen sink and wash your hands in warm water. The only way to understand what a comfort this was was to wash your hands in the cold water coming directly from the pump.

In some of the worst drought years, as many as six neighbor families got their drinking water from our well. And a couple of dry winters, when the water in the cistern got low, after a big snow we boys and our father shoveled snow into the cistern to build up the supply.

We didn't drink the cistern water, but our mother always felt that she was extremely fortunate in having the soft water for washing and for our baths.

After the clothes were washed and "frozen dry," our mother—it is difficult now to recall that she was a young woman at the time—had the ironing to do. Here, again, there have been wonderful improvements. She first used solid irons with iron handles. Then my father bought her a set of three irons with a detachable wood handle. She could have two irons heating on the kitchen range while she was busy with one on the iron board.

This system wasn't too bad in the winter, when the warmth of the stove was welcomed, but the same one also had to be used in hottest weather. The only way to get the irons hot in the summer was to have a hot fire in the stove. There were no electric fans, so my mother—and all others—sweated it out.

Later on, as a Christmas present, my father bought our mother a gasoline iron. This was a rather clumsy affair which had a small round reservoir for holding the gasoline, which was burned to keep the iron hot. Its only advantage was that the hot kitchen-range fire was eliminated. Whenever any gadget became available that would ease our mother's chores, my father bought it.

When we washed at home in the summer, our mother utilized the hand-powered washing machine. This machine had a lever on it that you pushed back and forth, "millions" of times, to activate the device inside that swished the clothes back and forth. For some reason, we boys just didn't have the strength to stick with it throughout the whole washing and our mother would have to take over.

Often, our mother would hire Grandma Davis, a large, elderly Negro woman, either to help with the washing or to do the washing herself. If Grandma Davis came to our house, she either washed on the board or pushed and pulled the lever on the washing machine. To us, this was proof that on a washing machine women just have more strength and endurance than boys.

Grandma Davis made a living "taking in washing" and helping young mothers with housework after the birth of babies.

When Grandma Davis did the washings at her own home, she washed on tubs in her back yard. Among the most pleasant occasions of the summer for our family would be taking the washing to Grandma Davis's house on a Sunday evening. We'd load the wicker basket of clothes on our coaster wagon and the whole family would walk the quarter of a mile down the dirt road to her little house. We always visited for a while, because everybody liked Mrs. Davis. She was supposed to have been the daughter of slaves, but I never heard the whole story. At some time, there must have been a "Grandpa Davis," but I never heard him mentioned.

Grandma Davis charged a dollar to do the washing and she needed the money.

My recollections of washday brought to mind many other incidents which indicate the improvements in living that women have seen, most of which were experienced by our mother in her lifetime.

As an example, I can remember Mother commenting on how long it always took Aunt Lou Romick to get ready to go somewhere. Aunt Lou (a close family friend) was a pretty and fastidious young farm wife. She'd always take lots of time to bathe—in a galvanized tub because there was no other kind—put on her good dress and then she'd hitch Old Dick to the buggy. After harnessing the horse, she'd go back into the house to wash her hands again. My mother always contended she could save time by harnessing Dick first and then taking her bath. I'll wager neither my mother nor Aunt Lou realized that I overheard them talking about this little matter and would remember it nearly 60 years.

Aunt Nellie (a real aunt) drove Old Speck to the Ladies Aid and Scotch Birthday Club meetings. Speck was a fine, big sorrel, a wonderful buggy horse, but he had one bad trait. When the meetings were over and all the ladies were getting into their buggies, anything, or maybe even nothing, could excite Speck and he'd stand straight up on his hind legs in the buggy shafts. It always looked as if he were going to fall over backward into the buggy seat. This was a frightening experience for man or woman and everybody always was glad when Speck calmed down and was ready to trot merrily home.

Young mothers today who complain that they operate delivery services for their families as they haul the kids here and there in their cars can at least be happy that they don't have to hitch a horse to a buggy for each trip.

Back to the house—we, of course, didn't have a vacuum cleaner. So, periodically, the rugs had to be hung over the clothesline and the dust knocked out of them with a beater, a wire device with a wood handle that looked something like a tennis racket. This was great fun for awhile. The dust would rise in clouds and each hard crack with the beater would sound like an explosion. But here again, boys' arms just couldn't take it for long. Our mother would have to take over.

Remembered, too, are the evenings at home when it seemed our mother was always darning stockings. We boys wore the long, black kind that came over the knees and were held up by garters. These stockings always had holes in the toes, the heels and at the knees. During World War I, when all things were scarce, our mother ordered stocking feet from a mail-order house, and these were sewn on the legs of stockings when the original foot part had worn out.

Undoubtedly, these were the ugliest things that

boys ever had to wear. We don't have young children at our house anymore, but something must have happened to eliminate the stocking-darning chore as I no longer see women doing such work.

Of course, for any work done at night, a light was necessary. It was a daily chore at our house to clean the chimneys on the coal-oil lamps. This could be done using a piece of newspaper to wipe out the soot that gathered inside the glass chimney. The lamp had to be filled with coal oil and the wick trimmed. Without this trimming, the lamp would smoke. All this was part of a woman's daily work.

The lamp had another use, too, beyond providing light. Our mother had a little device called a hair curler which could be heated by sticking it down into the lamp chimney when the light was burning. By rolling her hair on the heated iron, she could create a curl. Nobody had even heard about a permanent wave or a beauty parlor.

I almost forgot butchering. Since we didn't live on a farm, we'd have some farmer kill a hog for us and bring us the carcass to process. This meant hours of cutting hunks of fat into little pieces to be boiled into lard. What a mess for the kitchen. I'll admit the fresh pork and pancakes were a delight for breakfast, but I'm sure our mother was glad when we gave up getting our meat "wholesale."

Not to be forgotten either was the fact—on that zero morning—that our "bathroom" was 80 feet from the kitchen door, and outdoors.

Mud Is Still Mud

38

In some years, mud gets national attention for a real economic reason. Rain and snow which make fields muddy can delay the harvest of hundreds of millions of bushels of corn, soybeans and grain sorghums valued at hundreds of millions of dollars.

Mud, obviously, can be an important factor in the economy of this country even in these modern days when most of us seldom ever get off the pavement. But mud was a part of life for every person, the home, the farm and the community when I was a boy growing up.

This was before we had any paved roads in our community. Kids walked to school down muddy country roads. Housewives hung up their clothes to dry on lines in muddy back yards. The family milk cow (or cows) stood knee deep in mud in her pen. You walked through mud to the wood pile to get fuel for the kitchen range or the big round stove in the front room. At most country homes, you walked in mud on the path that led to the outdoor "toilet."

We were fortunate in our house at Maple Hill. We had a sidewalk that led to the coal house where we kept corn cobs (for kindling to start the fire), wood and coal, and to the three-hole outdoor toilet (two holes were adult size while the third was a little box-like affair for the smallest youngsters).

We had our dry weather at Maple Hill, too, of course, but in the winter, generally, when the ground wasn't frozen, you could count on mud. So we did.

As an example, every home was equipped with some kind of shoe or boot scraper at the back door.

"Don't you boys forget to scrape your shoes," was a common call to hear from Mother when she heard footsteps at the door.

The best scrapers were those my father made at his blacksmith shop. They were made of iron on the anvil. In general, they were shaped like a wide "H," with the two prongs set in concrete to give them a sturdy base. Some were more elaborate with the upper parts of the prongs on either side curved outward. All, of course, had the blade on which to scrape off the mud.

Makeshift scrapers were made of any kinds of pieces of metal, such as a broken disk or a plow blade.

At school we had a large scraper made with a bar across the top so that youngsters could hold onto this bar while they were standing on first one foot and then the other in the scraping process.

Another piece of equipage at every home was a gunny sack on the back porch on which you could also wipe your shoes. Gunny sacks (burlap) were used everywhere for cleaning off mud. We used them in the blacksmith shop, as an example, in cleaning the mud off horses' hooves and ankles before they were shod.

Try as you would, it was difficult, particularly on the farm, to get the mud off your shoes completely, even with the scraper and the gunny sack. Most men and big boys, therefore, wore rubber boots. After cleaning off the mud the best they could, they'd remove the boots on the back porch and walk into the house in their sock feet. Our mothers in those days didn't like muddy floors any more than they would today, although as far as I can recall nobody—not anybody—then had wall-to-wall carpeting.

In bad weather it was not considered impolite or uncouth for a man or the bigger boys to lounge around the house in their sock feet. Everybody, especially housewives, regarded this as common sense. And nearly all boot socks were made of a heavy gray wool or a light brown cotton with white feet. Some factory must have made them by the millions, because that was about all you could buy at the stores.

Rubber boots, while entirely appropriate for mud, were about the coldest thing you could wear unless you did have on heavy socks and even then, once they were cold clear through, your feet nearly froze. This was why it was such a pleasant experience to shed the boots at the back door and then put your sock feet into the close proximity of the heat either from the open oven in the kitchen or the Round Oak stove in the front room.

Women and girls wore buckled overshoes, but if the

264

housewife had to make a hurried trip to the wood pile, feed the chickens, gather the eggs or maybe if she were helping with the milking, she'd slip into one of the pairs of boots on the back porch. It wasn't the most stylish get-up for a woman, but under the circumstances, who cared?

The worst thing about milking in rainy weather was the mud on the cow's legs and the ball of mud that so often accumulated on the end of her tail. She could swing that tail like a sledge hammer to clobber you on the shoulder or side of the head.

Even in the relative coziness of the barn, milking a muddy cow was not the sanitary process that it is today. The cow in those days didn't walk through a shower of warm water to remove all dirt, nor was her udder rinsed with warm water and dried with a clean paper towel. The most meticulous milkers would take a bucket of water with them to the barn to wash the cow's udder but, generally, on a cold winter day, the milker squirted a little warm milk into his hands, wiped the teats as best he could and started milking.

It would be difficult to find a better example of progress in sanitation than that which has been accomplished in our modern dairies as compared to the process followed in the cold, drafty barns on the old-fashioned farm or little town barn lot.

Mud interfered with the harvests in the days of teams and wagons, just as it does today with the advanced self-propelled combines. In the days of hand shucking of corn, however, the farmer didn't expect to complete his harvest in a few days. Often he shucked corn as he needed it to feed the hogs all winter long.

265

But a farmer couldn't shuck corn if the fields were heavy with mud or if the shucks were wet even when he was throwing the ears into a wagon drawn by a team of big horses. The shucks wouldn't snap from the stalks when they were wet and it was too messy for both man and horses when the ground was muddy. Farmers then waited, just as they do now, for the ground either to dry or freeze.

Shucking corn by hand on a freezing day was a frigid task. Farmers wore flannel mittens with two thumbs. Either side of such mittens served as the palm. Perhaps the coldest job of all was driving back to the barn after the day's work was done. Working in the field, the farmer could keep warm from exercise. On the trip back to the barn, he would walk beside his team, the lines tied together and across his shoulders, while he clapped his hands together in an effort to keep the blood circulating and warm.

Many farmers shocked their corn in the fall, either cutting it by hand with a corn knife or with a corn binder. In either case, with the corn in the shock, the husking process could proceed as the farmer chose throughout the fall and winter. Nearly all farmers in those days fed all the corn they raised, thus there was no urgency to get the grain shucked and to the market. Corn in the shock kept almost as well as in the bin.

The shocks made great havens for cottontail rabbits and were favorite hunting places for me, my brothers and neighboring boys. Our dogs easily could dig their way into the corn shocks to rout out the rabbits.

Nowadays it is difficult to find a shock of corn because nearly all of it is cut with a combine which

266

both picks the corn from the stalk and shells it from the cob. More than half the corn harvested is sold from the farm today. Since crops are so much larger than 40 or 50 years ago, more corn is sold than used to be harvested in total. Therefore, because more corn actually is moved from the farm, mud interferes to a greater extent than before.

Trucks were beginning to come into use when I was a boy, but, unfortunately, both they and motor cars preceded the good roads. Trucks, which originally came equipped with solid tires, were almost useless in heavy mud. The ranches at Maple Hill used big wagons pulled by strong horses and mules to haul corn and cottonseed cake to cattle on feed. In fact, it was a common comment in that day that the car and truck never would supersede the horse on the farm. People just couldn't visualize the improvements that were to come in both highways and machines.

Horses and mules pulling heavy loads on muddy and icy roads had to be well shod. Thus meant winter work in the blacksmith shop. If there was a period when the roads were rough and frozen, the ranchers would bring their work stock into the shop for sharp-shoeing, which meant putting long and sharp toe and heel caulks on the shoes. My father and grandfather fashioned the heel caulks on the anvil, but they welded on a heavy, sharp toe-caulk that came from a horse-shoe factory.

Good farmers and ranchers curried (brushed) their horses every day in muddy weather even though this added to the drudgery of the winter feeding task.

A chore I never had but one about which the local

267

farm boys complained perhaps more than any other was to go down to the pasture pond in the morning or in the evening and chop holes in the ice so the cattle and horses could drink. Obviously, this was a cold job and it was always a muddy job, too, because the feet of the animals could cut up the pond bank until it was a rough mess.

The general use of the motor car both emphasized the hazards and difficulties of mud but led to the conquering—for the most part—of this burden to mankind. It was the motor car, not the horse and buggy, that forced modernization of the roads and highways.

But at the start, muddy roads had the cars whipped. If the mud were bad enough, you just didn't try to go.

While we tended to stay off the roads when they were at their muddiest, there were times when this was impossible. It could and did snow or rain while you were away from home. A pair of chains were more necessary for mud than they were for snow today, and when I was a boy no one ever had heard of a snow tire.

Model T Fords were good mudders, but even they could get stuck so that you'd have to "borrow" a post from a nearby fence and pry your vehicle out of the deep ruts.

Worst of all, though, was getting so much gumbo mud packed between wheels and the underside of the fenders that the wheels couldn't move. This meant getting sticks, screwdrivers or any other gadget you could lay your hands on and hacking away at the mud

268

until you could get the wheel cleared.

When you got home, you couldn't get out the hose and wash the mud from under the fender and from the rest of the car for the simple reason that no hose would be there. In those days before electricity on farms and little towns, water from a hose was not an available luxury. The mud stayed on until it rained.

Most of the inconveniences of mud have long since passed, especially for those of us who live in cities or towns. Unless it is an antique or an ornament, you probably can't find a scraper in use at a single Kansas City home. And it has been a long time since any of us dug the mud from between the wheel and fenders of our motor cars.

But when you get away from the homes and the paved highways, when you get completely out-of-doors and into the fields where crops are grown under the canopy of only the sky, nature still controls. As experience so well demonstrates, mud can keep men's best and most modern machines from operating.

Despite all our progress, mud is still mud.

The Versatile Nail Keg

39

A FEW nights ago I noticed in a television show a nail keg was used as a chair in a farmstead scene. And I wondered just how many people would appreciate the appropriateness of this bit of rural atmosphere.

The keg was in a natural setting as far as I was concerned because we always had several of them sitting around in our blacksmith shop. In fact, in a barn, livery stable or any place where a fellow needed something handy on which to sit, a nail keg was just the thing. It was just about the right height. With a folded gunny sack on top, it was fairly comfortable.

Nobody worried in the least about getting it dirty or scratched, and if the steel bands came loose and the staves caved in, you just threw the old staves into the fire in the big round stove and got another keg.

We got kegs in my father's blacksmith shop in two ways. Tom Oliver had a carpenter and wagonmaker's shop in the rear of our building. Wagonmaking and blacksmithing were complementary trades. Old Tom occasionally got a keg of nails. Also, horseshoes came in the kegs on the local freight out of Kansas City.

In the winter when my father had a hot fire going in the pot bellied stove that warmed only a relatively small circle of the shop, the nail kegs would be formed in a ring within the heat's perimeter. Farmers in their overalls and heavy coats would sit on the kegs and visit while my father and grandfather were shoeing their horses.

On a Saturday morning, when the weather was bad, we boys would sit on the kegs near the stove and sharpen our pocket knives on whetstones. We'd put a drop of oil on the stones and whet the knives until they were sharp enough to shave the hair on our arms.

In the summer, shop customers could take the kegs to the big east door to sit in the afternoon shade while plow shares were pointed or cultivator shares polished.

The fact is, a nail keg had a versatility that made it ideal around the shop. Two kegs could be used as a sawhorse when you had a board to saw. You could stand on a keg to reach high into the bolt rack where my father kept many sizes of bolts and nuts.

If there are those who haven't seen a nail keg— frankly I don't know whether nails still are shipped in kegs or not—they are just small barrels, about two feet high and about 10 inches wide at the top and bottom. I'm sure you won't find them around the better stores and shops today.

Looking back, it seems to me safe to say that the

nail keg had its heyday in the pre-over-stuffed furniture age. Because, come to think of it, we just didn't have much overstuffed furniture in our country town, but we managed to enjoy sitting just the same. We had no overstuffed furniture in our house, but we did have a leather couch. A few persons had what were called Morris chairs which had padded seats and backs. For easy sitting, most people used rocking chairs.

Outdoors, we did a lot of improvising. For example, when the first motor cars began to wear out, the removable leather-covered seats somehow found their way to front porches of farm houses and one was given a spot in front of the garage in our town. Two men could lounge on one of these seats as they watched farmers in their buggies and wagons or Model T's come into town or watch the big red Standard Oil tank wagon drawn by four huge horses pull up to the garage with a load of gasoline for the garage's hand-pumped gasoline facilities.

Across the street in the town's two general stores there were revolving stools at the dry goods counters where women from town and the farm gathered on Saturday night to sit and visit. While the women folks were visiting inside, if it was a warm summer night, the men would be sitting on the stone seat built into the front of Jim Fyfe's restaurant and pool hall.

For the most comfortable sitting downtown, both Fyfe's restaurant and Jack Herron's barbershop had captain chairs, but on a busy Saturday night there wasn't room for all the men downtown in these two places. Incidentally, the blacksmith shop never was opened at night as a visiting place. If some farmer wanted to pay his bill, my father would open the doors temporarily and light a lamp or lantern while he filled out the check for the farmer to sign.

The elite place in town was the drugstore where there were iron-legged chairs around iron-legged tables with marble tops. You lingered on these chairs while you enjoyed a soda or sundae, but people didn't "loaf" at the drugstore tables.

The most uncomfortable chairs in all the town were at the depot. These were benches along the walls, divided by iron arm rests with the express purpose of making it impossible for anyone to lie down to sleep.

In those days the "bums" traveled the rails, not the highways. Often the country depot was the only place open all night with a fire going in a big stove. The bums or hoboes would have liked nothing better than to have stretched out on a comfortable bench for a warm night's sleep. The depot seats prevented this, forcing the erstwhile travelers to seek what warmth might be available in some farmer's barn.

But in their successful efforts to cope with the bums, the railroads also added to the discomfort of their own customers. Nothing was worse than waiting in the station hours for a late train to arrive. You'd try to lay your head on the iron arm rests, but nobody could stand that for long. Then you'd go outdoors and look hopefully down the track to the signal lights, hoping for the red lights (instead of the green for all clear) that would indicate the train's approach. Next you'd ask the station agent just one more time when the train would be due and he, obligingly, would ask Topeka, via his telegraph keys, for the latest word. If the train still hadn't arrived in Topeka, his sad report would be that "something must have slowed her down after she left Kansas City."

At the time I was a boy, at least, people didn't loaf inside the depot. But on a nice summer night we'd sit on the baggage truck at the station and wait for the night flyer from Kansas City to arrive.

The baggage truck was an iron-tired wagon which the station agent used to pull along the baggage cars for loading and unloading cream cans and other heavy items. It always was available as a place to sit—until just before time for the train to arrive. At that moment, the agent would order everybody off as he grabbed the handle on the wagon's tongue and pulled it into position to be abreast of the opened doors of the mail and express car.

People use to improvise "chairs" on the farm. The milk stool is a good example. Tradition usually displays this device as a small three-legged stool with a circular seat. However, most milk stools I saw around Maple Hill were considerably less pretentious. In fact, they were just two pieces of 2x4 nailed together in the shape of a T. You balanced yourself on one of these stools by sitting on it squarely, and leaning your head on the cow's flank.

Many a milk stool also has been used to whack Old Bossy on the rump after she gave milker, milk stool and milk bucket a side-winder kick that sent them sprawling.

Another outdoor seat made by farmers was a swing hung by long chains to a limb of a tree. It should be recognized that this was in the day before electricity

276

and air conditioning. The object for many of the improvised chairs, swings or hammocks was to have a place to sit outdoors where there was a good breeze.

Although our houses were comfortably furnished at Maple Hill for the time about which I write, we did a lot of improvising for chairs when company came. By company, I mean when relatives or friends arrived for dinner with lots of children.

At our house, for instance, we had a round oak dining room table and six chairs. We also had a kitchen table and a few straight chairs. We had the piano stool with a spinning seat which always would be turned as high as it would go for one of the youngsters. The family high chair went to a baby.

Almost every house, ours included, had a wash bench. This simply was a wooden bench on the back porch where the housewife could put two galvanized wash tubs.

When company came the wash bench would be brought inside where it served as an excellent chair for three or four children at the table. If a youngster was too small, our mother added a pillow so the child could reach his plate.

No matter how many came to dinner, we always found some kind of chair or bench for them to sit on, and the dinners were so good nobody ever complained about the informality of the chairs. We had to improvise because as I recall no one had bridge or folding chairs to take care of such emergencies.

Yes, if you see a nail keg used as a chair on a TV show, be assured that this is an authentic piece of furniture from a bygone era of rural America.

Many Ways
To Get Rid of Ashes

40

THE new and almost sudden emphasis now being put on coal for fuel and energy will help recall what was once an asset of considerable proportions in this country as well as a gross nuisance.

I refer to ashes.

When you burn coal, you get ashes. And then you have to do something with the ashes. This is something most of us have forgotten, and many of the younger generation never knew.

Fortunately, ashes did serve some good purposes.

Coal was the elite fuel in its heyday, at least in the rural areas, as contrasted to wood.

You bought coal and had it hauled to the coal shed or shoveled into the bin in your cellar.

To get wood, you had to saw or chop down a tree, saw the logs into stove lengths and then split the logs. Wood didn't last as long in the stove or furnace as coal did. It took a huge pile to last through the winter. The farmer and his sons usually tried to cut and stack a big pile of wood before the really cold weather set in. But if they didn't get the job done, it meant going back into the woods for more sawing and chopping in the cold.

And you had to have a big box in the kitchen where wood could be stacked dry and where it would always be available to keep the kitchen range going as the housewife cooked, washed dishes and did the family laundry.

Wood was "free" on the farm, if you put no value on labor, but as anybody who lived in those days will recall, you paid dearly for every thermal unit of heat that was provided. Unfortunately, the power saw hadn't been invented.

Just as soon as a farm family could afford it, it shifted to coal, and then, in more modern times either to propane gas or electricity.

In Maple Hill the lumber yard solicited all families early in the fall on their coal needs, then ordered two, three or four cars—whatever was required. When the cars arrived and were set on sidings near the Rock Island depot, men with lumber wagons shoveled the coal from the cars into their wagons and distributed it to the coal sheds in the back yards. A big bin at the lumber yard also was filled to take care of additional needs that might arise in the winter.

Bringing in buckets of coal each night was one of the chores that befell boys. The few cases where mothers did have to carry coal to the house were used as object lessons.

"Surely," my mother would say as did many others

of our friends, "you wouldn't want to see me lugging in a heavy bucket of dirty coal like poor old Mrs. Jones, would you?"

But, as bringing in the coal and the corn cobs for kindling was one of the daily chores for boys, so also was carrying out the ashes.

The kitchen range had an oblong metal box which caught the ashes from the fire chamber. You merely slid this box from the stove and carried it outside to dump the ashes.

To get the ashes from the Round Oak stove in the front room, you had to use a small shovel and dip the ashes from beneath the fire chamber into a bucket. The problem was to do this without getting ash dust all over the room. The stove was sitting on a square of zinc, but it was almost impossible to shovel ashes from the stove without just a little getting on the rug.

We had various places to dump the ashes outside. One was the driveway from the street to the garage.

Likewise, several square yards of the edge of the roadway in the front of our house was "paved" with ashes, giving a little better footing in the muddy weather to anybody alighting from a car or buggy.

The ashes always eventually worked down into the mud so there never was a surplus. You just kept adding on where needed.

At my father's blacksmith shop, ashes from the forge and the big iron stove around which farmers sat while waiting for work to be done or while just plain loafing, were spread in front of the building between the street and the main doors. The use of ashes through the years provided a footing that was in contrast to the muddy ruts in the street before sand and gravel eventually were applied.

On the ash apron at the shop's front door, farmers or my father would take a long iron scraper and scrape mud from the horses' feet before they were taken inside to be shod.

At our school, where there was one of the few furnaces about which Maple Hill could boast, Walt Glenn, the caretaker, took the ashes each morning to spread on the paths leading to the boys' and the girls' outdoor toilets.

The platform where passengers loaded and unloaded from trains at the depot was surfaced with fine, black ashes which the railroad brought in coal cars.

Coal and ashes were an integral part of the railroad business at that time when all the steam engines were fired by coal.

You couldn't get away from the ashes in the summer, even as a passenger.

Before air conditioning, when the weather was hot, passengers had to open windows on trains for at least a measure of comfort. Wealthy, first-class passengers riding in Pullmans could get fresh air by sitting on the back platform of the observation car at the end of the train. This was considered the last word in luxury among boys who used to stand with envy on the depot platform watching the fancy trains go by. Few of us ever had the opportunity to ride a Pullman.

However, observation car, parlor car or smoker car passengers all had to contend with tiny ashes (little cinders, we called them) that came out of the smoke stack of the big steam engine pulling the train.

281

On a hot day when the windows were open, you'd try to find a seat on the side where you wouldn't get the full blast of the engine's smoke and cinders.

At the end of such a ride on a hot day, passengers would have to wipe the dust from their faces as they alighted from the train. It was all a part of traveling in those days.

My most potent memory of a cinder incident on a train concerns a trip I was making back to my Maple Hill home soon after I had started to work as a reporter on *The Star* in Kansas City. I started home with a bad sore throat.

Seated next to me by the window on the train was another boy who, unluckily, got a cinder in his eye. He couldn't get it out and although I was a stranger, he asked me to help. We went back to the washroom where I rolled a handkerchief to a point and with great care, and in a very close contact, I managed to extract the tiny black speck from his eye. We went back to our seat, shared an orange, and at Maple Hill I got off while he went on west.

My sore throat was worse when I got home. My folks called the doctor.

I had the mumps.

I've always wondered if 10 days later that boy also had the mumps.

After I had been in Kansas City several years and married, my wife and I bought our first home in 1930, a small new bungalow. It had a coal furnace. Each fall, I'd buy either coke or Arkansas semi-anthracite coal, at a price around $11 a ton. Four tons would just about take us through the winter.

Here, again, we had to dispose of the ashes. We put them in two big tubs, and every week or so, a trash man, for a small fee, would haul them away. But even in Kansas City ashes served a good purpose. We had a basement driveway. Whenever there was ice or snow, I could spread a few shovels of ashes on the driveway and always get enough traction to get the car out. In fact, after we had installed a gas furnace, I was lost without ashes when icy weather arrived.

I don't know when gas first became available for furnaces in Kansas City. I do know that it was considered a luxury and we didn't think we could afford it when we first set up housekeeping. Prior to World War II, there were many like us, perhaps a majority of the families in Kansas City.

But gas was taking over, despite the cost. Family after family was "converting."

I recall distinctly one frigid morning as we were getting started to work at *The Star* when the late George Wallace, for many years *The Star's* Missouri correspondent, told the late C. H. (Pip) Thompson, then the Starbeams editor, and the late "Doc" Hartley, a feature writer, that he hadn't slept a wink.

"I just laid there all night," he told his fellow workers, "listening to that meter click."

Those were the days when we were beginning to get rid of coal and ashes by turning to gas.

It is difficult for me to imagine that we ever would have to return in the home to coal for fuel.

If we do, we'll have to find some place to put the ashes.

Railroads
Sustained Small Towns

41

THE revolution in passenger-train service occasioned by the take-over by Amtrak brought not a ripple of excitement nor any repercussions in my old home town. Maple Hill some years ago had lost its passenger trains and they've even torn down the depot, so it was fully aware of what other towns were thinking which were going through the experience for the first time.

But Maple Hill in the heyday of the passenger trains was a good example of how little towns lived on the commerce of the railroads. The town was located where it was to be on the mainline of the Rock Island. When I was a boy, everything the town had moved in and out by railroad. The railroad was the one business that functioned 24 hours every day.

Many little towns have died when declining rail service plus the advent of good highways more or less eliminated their reason for existence. Maple Hill,

284

partly because it happens to be just off I-70 highway, has continued to thrive and today has more people and more new homes than ever in its history. Even so, the vacant spot where the depot used to stand creates a note of sadness. Somebody ought to put up a monument or a plaque which would say, for instance, that this was the place where we all used to gather at 9 o'clock at night to watch No. 39, the Colorado Flyer, coming in from Kansas City and Topeka. Or this was the place where the family would gather to meet grandpa and grandma who were coming in for a visit. Too, this was the place where we'd stand to watch and cheer as the "soldier" trains went by in World War I. And this was the place where they'd lift the coffin from the baggage car when some one from Maple Hill had died in a Topeka hospital and the body was being brought home for the funeral.

Maple Hill had excellent train service. At one time 18 passenger trains went through the town every 24 hours, eight of them stopping regularly. Others would stop for Pullman passengers.

Time schedules changed occasionally, but generally No. 40 stopped at Maple Hill between 6 and 7 o'clock in the morning and headed east to Topeka and Kansas City. No. 12, going east, stopped at 2 p.m. It was the train I caught for Kansas City when I left home in 1922 to start work as a reporter for *The Kansas City Star.* I had worked all morning in my father's blacksmith shop that day. No. 36, which stopped at 7 p.m., was our evening train to Topeka and No. 24, scheduled for 4 a.m., was the early-morning train that would get you into Kansas City in time for business activities.

Coming from the east there was No. 35 at 10 a.m., No. 11 at 1 p.m., No. 39 at 9 and No. 23 at 1:30 a.m.

In addition to the passenger trains, a freight dubbed the "local" arrived each morning from the east and returned from the west in late afternoon. Since most of Maple Hill's freight arrived from the east, the morning local was the busiest.

Maple Hill's depot, painted the traditional red of the Rock Island facilities, had three rooms. First was the waiting room with its big pot-bellied stove in the center. Around the walls were wooden benches divided by iron arm rests which were spaced close enough together that a person couldn't lie down for sleep. This was done to keep hoboes from using the depot as a haven of rest on cold nights.

But it also served to make the benches uncomfortable resting places for people who were waiting for trains three or four hours late, which occasionally was the case. The railroads, as I recall, catered only to the immediate needs of its passengers with little thought about extra features of comfort.

Also in this waiting room was Maple Hill's only vending machine, a device which would, for the expenditure of a penny, deliver either a little box with two small pieces of gum or a little square of bitter chocolate. The offering never varied. We boys thought the price was high considering the size of the product and we bought only in an emergency.

The waiting room's only other facility was a timetable, a blackboard on which the station agent noted whether the trains would be on time or late. Everyone walking into the waiting room automatically looked at the timetable, smiled if the train for which they were waiting was "on time," groaned if it were marked for late arrival.

The second, or middle, room in the depot was the office of the station agent, where he dispensed tickets, operated his telegraph key and kept his books. This room had a bay window through which the agent could look up and down the tracks either east or west to observe approaching trains. Visitors were not supposed to loiter in the agent's office, but there always were a chair or two where certain privileged friends could while away the hours.

The third room was for baggage. Baggage waiting to be loaded onto a train or that which had been unloaded could be held safe and out of the weather there. It was unheated.

Maple Hill's activities in the morning began with the arrival of No. 40. The depot, incidentally, was several hundred yards from the business district and marked the southern extremity of the town. It always was a source of amusement when strangers asked, "Why did they put the depot way down there?" for us natives to reply, "To get it on the railroad."

Each morning, after No. 40's arrival, a postal employee, always an elderly man, would gather up the mail sacks that had arrived over night, put them in a two-wheel cart and haul them to the postoffice in town. George Veale, a man with only one arm, had the job for years, as did Dad Leonard. Hauling the mail to the postoffice was considered a part-time job and the pay was $25 a month. As I recall, two trips each way each day were required.

When the mail had been delivered to the postoffice, the postmaster would hurriedly distribute the local mail into numbered boxes and that for farmers would be given to the two rural carriers who operated out of Maple Hill. These carriers would have their teams and mail carts waiting at the back door.

Meanwhile, townspeople would be gathering in the postoffice's waiting room. There was no house-to-house delivery. Old men started early to walk to the postoffice for their mail. It was part of a daily ritual.

W. J. Tod, one of the big ranchers would arrive either in his buggy, drawn by two sorrel geldings or astride his bay riding horse. H. G. Adams, the community's other big rancher, drove a pair of blacks. The ranchers picked up their own mail rather than waiting for the rural delivery.

My father would untie his leather apron, lay it over the anvil at the blacksmith shop and hurry to the postoffice about 8 a.m. which normally would be the time the postmaster would open the little window to the waiting room signaling the fact the distribution all had been made.

If there wasn't anything in your box by that time, you weren't getting any mail, a frustrating situation.

The mail included the morning papers from Kansas City and Topeka. The *Saturday Evening Post* came on Tuesday, *Colliers* magazine Friday. Sunday was a big day because of the arrival of the "funny papers."

After the early morning flurry over the mail, the next regular activity was the arrival of the local freight. The freight brought packaged groceries for the stores, the ice-packed freezers of ice cream for the

288

restaurant and drugstore, new plow shares and other farm equipment for the blacksmith shop, any heavy item that the local citizens had ordered from the mail-order houses.

Before motor trucks came in general usage, the operator of the local livery stable met the freight with his dray wagon to haul the items to their destinations in town.

Outgoing express each day included cans of cream destined for Topeka or Kansas City, crates of chickens and the empty ice cream containers being returned to the factories.

But the big business was heavy freight. It was not unusual for Maple Hill to handle hundreds of cars of cattle in a year, young cattle being brought in from the ranges of the Southwest for pasturing and feeding, fat cattle being shipped to market, mostly in Kansas City but some in Chicago. Additional hundreds of cars of wheat, corn and baled Prairie hay were shipped out each summer and fall.

More freight was handled out of Maple Hill, it was said, than from any other town on the Rock Island line between Topeka and Herington.

Dwight Cozad first served as a depot agent in the town in 1912 and regularly so engaged from 1928 until he retired in 1959. He recalled that it was nothing unusual for H. G. Adams to call on a Friday night or Saturday morning and put in an order for 30 to 35 livestock cars to be ready for Sunday evening loading. This always was an occasion for excitement, because the cattle would be driven by cowboys from the ranch to the stock pens at the railroad.

Amid much shouting they would be prodded up a chute into cars for overnight shipment to Kansas City, where they would be unloaded at the stockyards in time for the big Monday morning market.

Cozad was also a telegraph operator, as were all the station agents. The telegram was the quick means of communication with the outside world. Other than railroad orders and business transactions carried on by the ranchers and the Stock Growers State Bank, most telegrams for the rest of us were of an emergency nature. Generally, we dreaded receiving a telegram because so often it meant some relative or friend had died.

The station agent, by the code of the railroad, never divulged what was in a telegram until he could deliver it personally to the recipient named.

The depot agents worked three "tricks" of eight hours each. The first trick was from 7 a.m. until 3 p.m.; second trick 3 p.m. until 11 p.m. and the third trick 11 p.m. until 7 a.m.—seven days a week. The third trick was a lonely task and often meant that the agent was the only man awake in town in the depth of the night. But one thing was significant. As Cozad recalled, the station never was robbed.

Before the motor car came into general use, we in Maple Hill used the passenger trains almost like busses are employed in cities for commuting, mostly to Topeka. If we boys needed new suits for school, our mother would take us on No. 40 to Topeka in the morning to shop the stores on Kansas Avenue in the capital city. In the evening, if there were a good show at the Grand Theater in Topeka, sometimes three or four couples would take No. 36 to the city, returning after midnight on 23. The fare was two cents a mile or 42 cents.

One of the tragedies in our town in my boyhood days was the death after a brief illness of Delbert King, the son of a local doctor, at age 11 or 12. Mrs. King asked a group of Delbert's friends to be pallbearers. It was summer and I didn't have dress shoes, so I went to Topeka on No. 40, returned at 10 on No. 35 and wore my new shoes to the funeral that afternoon.

When anyone took a long trip on the train, it was standard practice to take a luncheon carried in a shoe box. We knew there were dining cars on the trains, but I never stepped into one until after I had been in Kansas City a few years.

My father bought our family's first motor car in 1916. It was an Overland. This was about the time the Model T's began to appear in droves. We were not the first to have a car. H. G. Adams bought a Cadillac, the Sells family bought a Hupmobile, Grant Romig a Dodge.

People began to arrive at the postoffice in cars instead of on horseback to pick up their mail. But it was to be a long time before the motor cars were to supersede the railroad for passenger traffic, largely because of the poor roads.

But, as Cozad recalled, when every family in town and every farmer got a motor car, the handwriting was on the wall for the eventual demise of the passenger train for service to little towns. The station agent could go days without selling a ticket.

Mile-long freight trains still roll down the tracks

with a long toot on the whistle at the Main Street crossing, the only recognition of the fact they are passing Maple Hill. The Rock Island is using the old side tracks at Maple Hill for the storage of junk boxcars. The passenger train era definitely is over for this little town along with many others.

Probably the trains themselves are not missed very much. This says a lot about why they are gone. But the weeds growing where the old depot used to stand have significance for those of us who remember when this was the busiest place in town. The next generation may not even know what a depot was.

Cautious Courting

42

EIGHT of us were seated around a table at a downtown restaurant when I heard one friend across the way say facetiously to another:

"This guy Turnbull is always writing about his home town, Maple Hill, and he tells about the fishing, hunting, Halloween, the blacksmith shop and Buffalo Mound, but he never mentions girls. Do you suppose there was no romance in Maple Hill?"

I was supposed to overhear the conversation, obviously; so I commented that when I was growing up in that little Kansas town the number of boys and girls was approximately equal—not very many of either— and we managed to get along normally. However, when it comes to writing about it, well, romance is better told in fiction. These Maple Hill stories have been true reminiscenses, not even fictitious names. Also, while I think I was about average, I'm sure I didn't cut a very wide swath, and the few that did—well, most of them are still around.

Another thing, I had not quite reached my 18th birthday when I left Maple Hill for Kansas City. Most of the time for serious courting was yet ahead. In fact, in our high school graduating class all eight were still single when we got our diplomas.

As teenagers, we had our fun and also a few worries, usually occasioned by a lack of sophistication that was both an asset and a liability. For instance, there was the time a new family moved to town with a daughter 14 or 16 years who was about the prettiest newcomer Maple Hill had seen. She had dark, curly hair and unusually big brown eyes.

Someone saw to it the first Sunday evening that the new girl attended Christian Endeavor at church. And one of the mothers, who was a leader, suggested that it would be nice if I would walk home with her.

The new family had moved into a house in the north part of town and it was a relatively long walk. Frankly, this was one of the high points of my career. Through circumstances which I had not had to promote myself, I had managed to have a "date" with the town's newest girl.

Next morning I went to school highly elated and expecting to get proper acclaim. Instead, I found that everybody in town already had learned that I had been a dud. It seems I had walked on the wrong side of the sidewalk the entire long trip to the girl's home.

It was the first time I knew a sidewalk had two sides. But the young lady was aghast. It was very embarrassing. She had no idea boys in Maple Hill were so lacking in courtesy that they'd let a girl walk on the outside.

This incident was typical of me—and I think of some of the other boys of the time, but not all—and also typical of a little town where little things could be awfully important. We were, I must admit, terribly bashful, but willing to learn.

As for the little town—it was amazing how news got around. Practically everybody knew what everybody else did. At least, this was the case once upon a time, and it wasn't all bad. I don't know how it is now. Why, today, they even have dial telephones.

Back in the days of the party line, there was none of this talking by the hour on the telephone. Sometimes folks along the line visited a little, but a boy and a girl didn't talk a lot of nonsense, not unless they wanted to put on a show for the whole countryside.

You'd call a girl and ask hurriedly if she had a way to the party. If she said she hadn't, you'd suggest you'd likely be by and she'd say that would be fine. That was it.

The fact is, we seldom used the telephone to make a date. One of my best friends, for instance, just wouldn't call a girl on a telephone. Sometimes if we had failed to make all arrangements at school, he would cajole me into making the call for him.

Most of the time, dates weren't formally arranged at all. We'd just meet. This was the reason we all went to Christian Endeavor (next to the fact it was a church service of course).

Several of the girls from farms roomed in town while attending high school. Roads were so bad they couldn't go back and forth to their homes. So, late Sunday afternoons their folks would bring them into town for the week, and the girls would go to Christian Endeavor. So also did the town girls and boys.

After services, the girls would start home in a group. We boys would follow. First thing you'd know some boy would be walking alongside a girl. Another would manage to do the same thing and eventually, we'd be walking in pairs. It just seemed to turn out that way.

Occasionally, one or two of the boys would have their parents' car and they'd take one or two couples to the late picture show at St. Marys, Kansas, 10 miles away.

Not all of us were allowed to do this. In the first place, it meant being up late, and secondly, not all our parents believed in Sunday night movies, even if you went to Christian Endeavor first.

Birthdays and similar occasions provided reasons for parties. In order to have a crowd, everybody always was invited. If the family had a phonograph we could dance; if not we played games—always the same games.

One of them was called "winkum." The girls sat in chairs in a large circle. Boys stood behind the chairs. One chair was vacant. The boy behind that chair would look slyly around the circle and then wink at some girl. She was supposed to jump quickly from where she was sitting to his empty chair. The boy who was standing behind her chair was supposed to grab her if he could to keep her from getting away. If he lost, he was "it" the next time.

Seems like a silly game now, but it had its moments.

No matter how elaborate the plans for the party, we always ended up with the same refreshments—hot cocoa with a marshmallow floating in the cup, and cookies. To have had ice cream would have called for making a freezer full or ordering one from Topeka. You didn't do that in the wintertime.

We had a card game we played, but it wasn't really "cards." This game was called somerset or Some-Are-Set. The cards had names and numbers and the rules were similar in many ways to regular playing card games; but since the cards were not the standard variety, it was all permissible. In a good many homes, including my own, a deck of cards just wasn't allowed.

We played somerset at parties, in small gatherings in the evenings at homes, and even at school during recess. The teachers played, too.

We played flinch and authors, too, but somerset was the favorite.

Incidentally, since our school had no gymnasium, any time we had to stay inside our recreational activities had to take place in the same room where we studied and held class. The same held true for school parties, except when we took over the basement which, while it held no desks, wasn't too attractive.

One thing that could foul up a high school party was the town boys. Any boy became a town boy immediately upon graduation from high school. These boys often wanted to date the high school girls, even though they never were invited to school parties. And some of the girls preferred the older boys. This meant hard feelings. As I recall, most of the Maple Hill girls upon graduation went to college to become school teachers.

We were having the junior-senior class party in the basement of the school one early May evening. This was always the elite event of the year. We had paper streamers tied from the corners of the room to crisscross above the long table. The girls had made place cards and we had colored napkins. Everything was so nice most of us were ill at ease.

The last course had been served and we were seated around the table with as much formality as we had ever attained when we heard noises in an adjoining little room which held the janitor's brooms, mops and other supplies. We suspected right away it wasn't mice. Some town boys were trying to crash the party.

Joe McClelland and I grabbed a fire extinguisher from the wall, turned the nozzle and started pumping. The stream of chemically treated water poured into the little room. We heard some one shout "Chloroform," and whoever was in there piled out a window, just as they had entered.

From then on we had a good time at the party. Formality was gone and we were back in a normal state.

Getting the family car was an achievement. Most parents would let us have the cars if there was a party at a farmhouse in the country which was too far away for walking, but it was difficult to get the vehicle just for riding around. It was a real privilege to have the car on Sunday afternoon; girls realized this, too. There weren't too many places to go, but it was fun just riding around a country square and going down Main Street each time.

Our cars all had muffler cut-outs which could be opened or closed by a lever that came through the floor board. We drove alternately to make the motor roar or to make it purr. The latter was accomplished by driving as slowly as possible so that you could hear each cylinder firing individually.

It took expert tuning to make a car run at that pace and we all thought we were mechanics. The girls maintained it was marvelous the way we handled cars—at least that is what they said.

The time came when I was graduated from high school and this put me in the town boy category. It sort of changed things and was one reason why so many young fellows headed for the city if a job wasn't readily available.

After being in the city awhile, it was nice to get back to the old home town to meet high school friends again. I got back one Friday night and immediately called long distance to another community where a girl I had dated in high school lived with her parents on a farm. I asked the operator for the farm home. I wanted to ask the young miss to go to a dance Saturday night at another nearby town.

There was a considerable wait. Finally the girl answered and in a few words told me she was sorry, but was busy.

The rural mail the next morning brought me a letter from the girl in which she accepted my invitation to the dance and also explained her refusal the night before. When I had put in my telephone call, the operator in her community, who also had been a student in our high school, recognized my voice. She knew I didn't want to talk to the girl's parents and she also knew the girl was having supper that evening with the family of a young farmer. She had been dating this fellow rather regularly since she had finished high school the previous May.

So, taking the matter in her own hands, the operator just completed the call to the young man's home. On the spot, the girl had to tell me "no," but she got her letter written in time to catch the rural carrier the first thing in the morning.

The next day I went back to Kansas City and she later married the farmer. This was so long ago that when he reads this I'm sure he'll do just as I have done many times—smile at the service you got from the country town telephone operator in those days. At least I hope this is the way he reacts.

Luncheon Circuit Notes

43

In my 48 years as a newspaperman I listened to a lot of speeches. Attending meetings is part of a reporter's job. And since it is part of his job he is, in effect, paid to listen to the speeches.

As a paid listener, it is entirely likely that the reporter may appraise a speech differently from others in the audience who may be there for entertainment, to learn certain facts or just to pass the time away. In the first place, the reporter hopes the speaker will say something that will be of interest to people who are not at the meeting as well as those in attendance. More specifically, he hopes to get a story for his paper. As I mentioned, that is what he's paid for.

Of course, not all of a reporter's time is spent listening to speeches, even in the agricultural field. He may, for instance, be writing about the Southern corn blight which is ruining a crop.

During my relatively long career in the newspaper business, I developed my own way of categorizing speakers, both good and bad.

Among good speakers, I put at the top the fellow who really had something to say that the audience wanted to hear. He might have been reporting on some new scientific development, telling a group of businessmen how to avoid tax troubles, explaining to women the symptoms of cancer, enlightening farmers on the intricacies of the farm program or a thousand and one other subjects. But the fact was, he had important information or facts to impart.

In such cases, it didn't really matter whether he had good delivery or stage presence as long as he could be heard. People had come to hear what he had to say, not how he said it.

Next there was the speaker who didn't have much to say, but did it so well people were impressed. I classified him as a good speaker, but not quite the equal of the man who had the important message.

Finally, among the good speakers, was the fellow who could tell one good story after another, while weaving in a few verities about motherhood, the virtues of hard work, saving your money and recognizing that good old America is the best country in the world no matter what.

Such a speaker left the audience elated. They couldn't recall exactly what he had said, but whatever it was, it sounded extremely interesting.

"You really should have been there," they'd tell others.

For audience preference, I'd have to put speakers of

this type above all others. They made no copy for the newspaperman, but I'd have to admit I liked them. I also was impressed by the fact that speakers with this ability were in such demand that they got paid—in substantial amounts.

In my category of poor speakers there was the man who had nothing to say and couldn't say it. He was followed by the fellow who had no message, but thought he was a second William Jennings Bryan or Billy Graham. And finally, there was the speaker who couldn't tell stories, but thought he had to, so he dragged out every old one in the book.

As the years began to pile up on me in my newspaper work, I began to get requests that I speak, a task for which I was neither prepared nor trained. But knowing how difficult it often was for the program chairman to get someone to fill a spot, I occasionally acquiesced, with some trepidation. As a result, I learned to speak just about as we boys learned to swim at Maple Hill, Kansas. The older boys would throw a younger one into a deep hole in Mill Creek and after considerable and frantic threshing about, he'd paddle out. You didn't learn to swim well under this system, but you could save yourself from drowning.

In my appearances, I attempted a combination of the speaker who had something to say and the one who could tell stories. Following the advice of a University of Missouri professor, I made an effort to use my stories to illustrate a point. Also, so I wouldn't forget, occasionally I made a series of notes on the things I was to cover in my talk, and now and then actually prepared an entire text. After each talk, I'd place my notes or text into a big envelope, hoping that if I were requested to talk again I could use the same copy. It seldom happened.

Upon my retirement from *The Star* December 31, 1970, I took with me a big box containing a pile of the old envelopes filled with the notes. It wasn't long before a civic club president called to ask if I would speak at a noon luncheon.

"What about?" I asked.

"We'd like for you to reminisce," he proposed.

Wondering in my own mind what I'd reminisce about, I thought I might get some clues from my notes on the old speeches. I started to thumb through them and this turned out to be an interesting experience.

I had neglected, I learned, not only to date the notes but to indicate where the talk had been made. Also, as I read the notes and even the texts, they seemed incredibly dull. What intrigued me most was the reminders of stories, such as "use the preacher story here."

What preacher story?

Several times, I had penciled in "Story of Brigham Young and the Indian with one leg." That must have been a good story or I wouldn't have used it more than once. It was the same way on "Story of the old lady on the train." I know they got laughs at the time, but now I couldn't recall a thing about them.

It was beginning to be a frustrating venture. How could such good stories fade from the scene entirely? Then, finally, I came upon a note which struck a familiar chord. It was "the shift story." This wasn't so long ago. Remember when young women began to wear the shift dresses, the kind that hung straight down from the shoulders? I think this was in the early 1960s. The story, told to illustrate the point that you can't always make up your mind from first appearances, was about a young man who arrived at his girl friend's home to take her to a dance.

She met him at the front door dressed in one of the new shift dresses.

Startled, he exclaimed, "Honey, are you just in style or are we in trouble?"

Encouraged by this experience, I began to make a game of checking the notes and trying to remember the stories. Sometimes I'd win. For instance, there was the anecdote about the preacher whose church wasn't doing well. But he thanked the Lord that the other two churches in town weren't doing very well either. The story illustrated a point on relative importance.

Then there was the story about the little boy returning home from school who was greeted by his mother:

"And what did mother's little darling learn in school today?"

To which he replied:

"I learned two boys not to call me mother's little darling."

I couldn't recall the moral of that story, but I did remember my note on "you tell 'em" used to illustrate the fact that it could be more difficult than you might think to convince someone to do something.

As this story went, when Oklahoma became a state, the constitution adopted permitted a man to have just one wife as was the case in all other states. But, as the story contended, some Indians had more than one, including a chief who had four. A law officer informed the chief about the new situation, but nothing happened. Finally, he called on the chief personally, explained the situation under the new laws thoroughly and told the Indian he would just have to get rid of three wives.

"Pick out the wife you want to keep," the lawman advised. "Then tell the other three they've got to leave, vamoose. It's the law."

"You tell 'em," the old chief said.

Thumbing more pages, here was the note, "Story of the daughter who obtained an osteopath for her mother." I wondered what that could have been. Sounded interesting. And next, "Story of two drunks on the railroad track." I know that must have been good. How could I forget them?

But this was followed by a familiar note, the story about the man falling into the grave. I told this story many times but finally quit using it because I was hearing it at too many other meetings. I used the story back in the early 1950s when the controversy was raging over flexible as against fixed price supports for farmers. I was emphasizing that high price supports tended to greater production and surpluses, that hardly anything is a greater incentive than money. There were some other incentives, of course, as could be illustrated by the man who fell into the grave.

This fellow, a workman, was saving time on his way home late one day by walking through a cemetery. He came to a newly dug grave and with normal curiosity, stopped to peer into it. Loose dirt around the edges gave way and in an instant he found himself at the bottom of the pit. The workman did his best to climb out but found he just couldn't make it.

Being of a practical bent, he assured himself there'd be some one there early the next day to prepare for the burial. Also, he still had an apple in his lunch box and a little coffee in his vacuum bottle. So he made himself as comfortable as he could in a corner of the grave and prepared to spend the night.

Much later in the night, another man, lost, befuddled and, as they say, under the influence, was crossing the cemetery and he, too, fell into the open grave. Frantically, he tried to get out. He jumped with no avail, seeking to get hold of the edges of the earth. He screamed for help, but got no answers. Finally, in a frenzy, he was digging his fingernails into one earthen wall while trying to brace his feet on the other. Then he heard a voice from the far corner of the grave calmly saying, "You'll never make it."

But he did.

Not in my notes was a story I never did tell because I considered it old hat when I was a boy. What always griped me was that the teller inevitably related the incident in the first person as if it actually had happened to him and his old pappy. To my disgust I heard this story told on TV just a few nights ago. I know you have heard it, but don't stop me now because I want to go on record as proposing this as a story that should be put in storage for at least a whole generation.

The way I heard it (as a small youngster) a boy came to school late and the teacher demanded an explanation.

"You wouldn't believe me if I told you," the boy contended.

"Just the same, let's hear your story," the teacher insisted.

"Well," began the boy, "it was this way:

"We'd been losing some chickens at our house and Papa had been trying to catch the thief, man or animal. Last night we were awakened by a noise in the henhouse so my papa slips out of bed with nothing on but his nightshirt, quietly steps onto the back porch where he takes his old double-barrel shotgun off the hook and heads out into the back yard.

"He cocked both barrels of that old blunderbuss and was creeping up on the henhouse kinda stooped over like but what he didn't realize was that Old Shep was creeping right along behind him. Just about the time Papa arrived at the henhouse door, he heard another noise inside and he stopped suddenly. But Old Shep didn't stop and his cold nose touched Papa on a place the night shirt didn't cover.

"And we've been cleaning chickens ever since."

Text in Intertype Century Schoolbook,
Titles in Century Schoolbook Bold
Printed on Warren's Olde Style
Designed by Ronald E. Garman
and David E. Spaw